D1166601

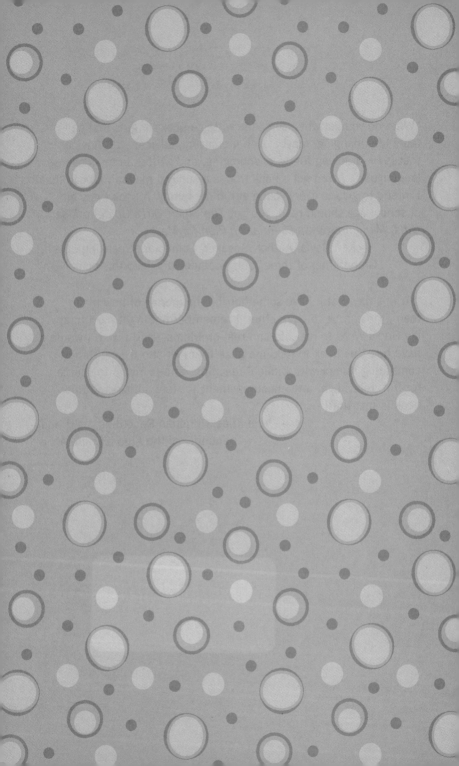

THE Smart Girl's GUIDE

TO **MEAN GIRLS, MANICURES, & GOD'S AMAZING PLAN** FOR **Me**

"BE INTENTIONAL" AND **100** OTHER PRACTICAL TIPS FOR **TEENS**

Susie Shellenberger & Kristin Weber

SHILOH RUN ▲ PRESS

An Imprint of Barbour Publishing, Inc.

Print ISBN 978-1-63409-713-0

eBook Editions:
Adobe Digital Edition (.epub) 978-1-63409-886-1
Kindle and MobiPocket Edition (.prc) 978-1-63409-887-8

Cover Design: Greg Jackson, Thinkpen Design

Kristin Weber author photo by Brian Maloney

The author is represented by and this book is published in association with the literary agency of WordServe Literary Group, Ltd., www.wordserveliterary.com.

Published by Shiloh Run Press, an imprint of Barbour Publishing, Inc., P.O. Box 719, Uhrichsville, Ohio 44683, www.shilohrunpress.com.

Our mission is to publish and distribute inspirational products offering exceptional value and biblical encouragement to the masses.

 Member of the
Evangelical Christian
Publishers Association

Printed in the United States of America.

To my sister Leah.
Thank you for suggesting I dedicate
the book to you.

-Kristin

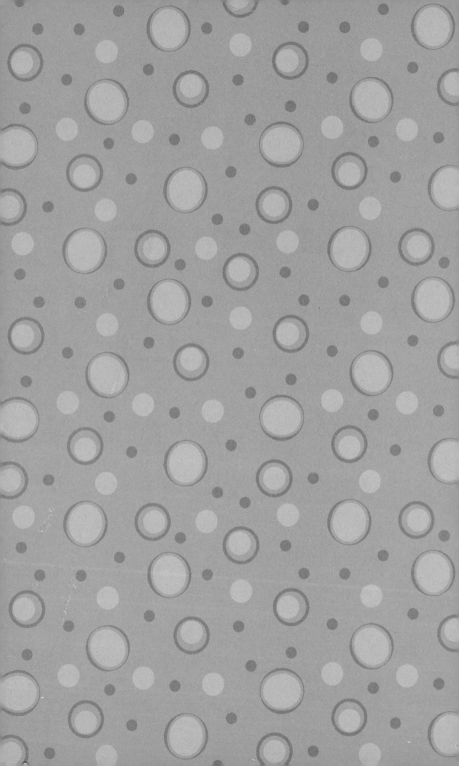

Contents

1.
Learn to Wait

We don't have to wait for much in our culture.

We can communicate to anyone at any time, have popcorn in three minutes, get custom-made food without leaving our car, watch television shows downloaded on demand to any device we want, and get most information at the click of a button.

The technological advancements of our time have made life much easier, but because of them we have lost the ability to wait. We want instant satisfaction and immediate results. Patience is no longer in our vocabulary.

We even want God to give us what we want instantly. Sometimes, though, God makes us wait for things. Since the beginning of the world, God has made His people wait.

He promised a Savior in Genesis 3, but He didn't send Jesus for thousands of years.

He made Abraham and Sarah wait many years after promising them a child through which all nations would be blessed. (Fun fact: Jesus came from the ancestry of Abraham, and every nation in the world was blessed by what He did for us on the cross. Pretty cool, huh?)

He made Joseph sit in jail for years for crimes he didn't commit before Pharaoh honored him with the position of second-in-command.

God uses these times of waiting to shape us. To prepare us. To mold us. To strengthen our character. To give us the ability to understand and empathize with people. To keep us from becoming spoiled. To bring us closer to Him. To give us rest.

God also uses these times of waiting for His own glory. As stories unfold and God shows up in seemingly impossible circumstances, we see more of who God is and learn more about His character. We realize that we are a small part of something much bigger than immediately getting our way.

Our timing is based on what we know now. God's timing is based on knowing **everything** in the entire universe: yesterday, today, and forever.

Waiting reminds us we aren't the center of the universe.

Waiting reminds us that God is in control.

Waiting reminds us that a day is coming when we will no longer wait. Our faith will become sight; sin will be no more, and we'll dwell in a perfect world with God.

-Kristin

• •

FROM GOD:

"And now, O Lord, for what do I wait? My hope is in you." (Psalm 39:7 ESV)

GO AHEAD—ANSWER:

→ What is something you've had to wait for? Was it worth it?

→ What are some other reasons God might make us wait for something?

→ Are you struggling to be patient? Ask God to help you trust in His timing.

FROM KRISTIN:

It takes patience to get patience, so be patient with yourself as you learn how to be patient. (See what I did there?)

FROM SUSIE:

Unless you're a hospital patient. Then you don't need to worry about being patient, because you can just sleep all day. (See what I did there?)

2.
Eliminate Distractions

Are you a basketball fan? I live in Oklahoma, and I'm a fanatic about our pro Oklahoma City Thunder team. I've been privileged to pray at a few of their home games, and when I do that, I'm given two free tickets and complimentary parking to the game. I love taking a friend and heading to downtown Oklahoma City to join the thousands of other fans screaming their loudest for the team.

Being inside the arena is a multisensory experience! Of course, there's the actual game to watch on the floor, but there are also a myriad of other things vying for the fans' attention: Rumble, the mascot; the cheerleaders; the flashing advertisements on the circular screens surrounding the top of the arena; T-shirts and giveaways being shot into the audience; the game on the giant screens; the camera shooting live shots of a variety of people in the audience; vendors selling food and drinks; and a multitude of smells, from baked pretzels to burgers to funnel cake fries; and on and on and on.

Even though I'm a fan, I've noticed that because of everything that's vying for my attention, it's easy to get distracted from the game itself. During those moments, I have to remind myself that I came to watch the game—not to get caught up in all the excitement that surrounds me. If I want to discuss the game the next day with friends, I need to stay focused on the main thing.

Let's carry this over into our spiritual lives. It can be easy for Christians to get distracted from the main thing: an intimate relationship with Jesus Christ. We can enjoy the trimmings of Christianity so much that it's easy to get so caught up in festivals, conferences, T-shirts, church parties, retreats, and clubs that our focus on Christ Himself tends to slip. We find ourselves zeroing in on the things *surrounding* Him instead of simply *Him.*

Discerning our distraction may be difficult, because the things fighting for our attention are actually good things! They often enhance our relationship with Him. But let's carry this to the extreme: if I attend a Thunder basketball game and get so carried away with the excitement of everything going on around me, I could actually leave without ever knowing the score. Sounds silly, doesn't it?

The same thing often happens spiritually. I've known some teens who have been so into Christian "stuff" that they've missed the actual Savior, Jesus Christ. They're excited about camp, car washes, feeding the homeless, and Bible quizzing, but when you ask them what Jesus is doing in their lives, they come up blank.

Let's keep the main thing the main thing. It has—and always will be—Jesus Christ Himself!

—Susie

. . . .

FROM GOD:

Let us run with perseverance the race marked out for us, fixing our eyes on Jesus, the pioneer and perfecter of faith. For the joy set before him he endured the cross, scorning its shame, and sat down at the right hand of the throne of God. (Hebrews 12:1–2 NIV)

GO AHEAD—ANSWER:

→ What easily distracts you from concentrating on Christ alone?

→ What can you do to become more focused on your relationship with Christ?

→ What is Christ currently teaching you?

FROM SUSIE:

Remember the Israelites from the Old Testament? God freed them from Pharaoh's evil rule so He could give them their own lush and fertile land. But the Israelites got distracted, and it took them more than forty years to get to the Promised Land. (Maybe it was because Moses was their leader; it's been said that men never like to stop and ask for directions!) If we'll remember to simply walk straight ahead and allow God to guide us, we'll get where He wants us to be much sooner.

FROM KRISTIN:

I don't get distracted very easily. Once I start something I focus until I. . .

3.
Know the Truth

Have you ever had a test with true/false questions on it? What's the easiest way to know what's false?

By knowing what's true. Because the fastest way to spot a lie is to know the truth.

There are many lies floating around in the world, some of them pretty convincing: "Jesus never claimed to be God." "You've sinned too much for Jesus to love you." "You're not worth anything." Those are all false statements that people will declare as truth.

If we're going to combat these lies, we must learn what's true. The best source of truth is the Bible, so let's see what the Bible has to say about each of the above statements.

When people doubted that Jesus was indeed both God and man, He told them, "I and the Father are one" (John 10:30 ESV). (That's one of many places in the Bible where Jesus claimed divine authority.)

When you think you've sinned beyond what you believe can be forgiven, know that God saved Paul, who murdered Christians for their faith. He also promises that anyone who confesses his or her sin is cleansed from all unrighteousness (1 John 1:9).

When you're tempted to believe you're not worth anything, remember that God cares about even the smallest birds and tells us, "Fear not, therefore; you are of more value than many sparrows" (Matthew 10:31 ESV). We're reminded later on that God proved how much He cherishes us by giving up His own Son to die for us.

–Kristin

· ·

FROM GOD:

"Sanctify them in the truth; your word is truth." (John 17:17 ESV)

GO AHEAD—ANSWER:

→ What are some lies that you've heard? How did you respond to them?

→ How well can you spot something false?

→ What are some things you can do to recognize truth?

FROM KRISTIN:

When I was a child, I used to do a lot of Where's Waldo puzzles. (Look him up if you've never heard of him.) The hardest puzzle was the last one, where you had to find the actual Waldo in a picture with hundreds of imposter Waldos. The better you knew the real Waldo, the easier it was to pick him out of the crowd of imposters.

FROM SUSIE:

So where is Waldo?

FROM KRISTIN:

It doesn't matter. He's not real.

FROM SUSIE:

So. . . Waldo died after you found him?

FROM KRISTIN:

No! He didn't die. He was just a game.

FROM SUSIE:

Hmm. I'm thinking maybe he's lost and we should start looking for him again.

FROM KRISTIN:

Maybe he's hanging with Carmen Sandiego. I never found her either.

4.
Anchor Yourself to the Truth

Let's put your truth-spotting skills to the test.

Here's a paraphrase of something I heard a pastor on television say recently.

"If you have enough faith, bad things won't happen to you. God wants you to be happy—but it's up to you."

What's wrong with this statement? Can you spot where this pastor might be leading people astray?

First, our level of faith doesn't determine what happens to us. Terrible things happen to very godly, faithful people. And wicked people sometimes live easy, luxurious lives. In fact, Jesus assures us we'll have trouble. Jesus was rejected and despised by people, and as His followers we can expect the same to happen to us. (I promise this will get more encouraging; just keep reading!)

The second statement, "God wants you to be happy," is confusing. God wants you to be *joyful*. Those are two different things. (For more on the difference between joy and happiness, see #13, "Be Slap Happy.")

Ask yourself the following questions:

1. Does this statement put control of my circumstances in my hands? Or does it encourage me to trust God's will?

2. Does the person saying this have a motive other than wanting to preach God's truth? (For example, is the person asking for money on the television?)

3. What part of the Bible supports this claim? Was the scripture used taken out of context?

Because there are so many false philosophies floating around, it's important for you not only to know the truth but also to anchor yourself to the truth.

How can you anchor yourself to the truth?

By knowing, believing, and practicing the Word of God.

Take every thought, philosophy, and claim captive to what you know is true. Sometimes we don't like what's true and we want to believe things that sound more enticing. Truth always wins, is always on your side, and is the best weapon against Satan's attacks.

If you're not sure, ask a parent, pastor, or someone who has a track record for speaking the truth even when it's not what people prefer hearing. This will help you strengthen your beliefs.

Finally, apply what you know is true to your life.

-Kristin

• •

FROM GOD:

But false prophets also arose among the people, just as there will be false teachers among you, who will secretly bring in destructive heresies, even denying the Master who bought them, bringing upon themselves swift destruction. (2 Peter 2:1 ESV)

GO AHEAD—ANSWER:

→ Can you think of any false teachings you've heard that sounded convincing? How did you spot the lie?

→ Can you know the truth without believing it?

→ What are some ways you can live out the truth?

FROM KRISTIN:

If you're not sure about something you've heard, pray in that moment and ask God to give you wisdom.

5.
Get Rid of Your Pet Hippopotamuses

In Africa more people are killed by hippopotamuses than by any other animal. (Betcha thought I made a mistake by saying hippopotamuses, huh? There are actually two accepted plurals of hippopotamus—the one I used and also hippopotami. Cool, huh? Now you can impress your friends. Of course, it would have been a lot easier if I had simply written hippos. But then you'd never know the above fun fact!

Hippos weigh around 7,900 pounds, and they're the third largest mammals on earth—right after elephants and white rhinos. Their hide alone can weigh half a ton. That's heavy skin! But just because they're big doesn't mean they're not fast. They can actually outrun humans. Hippos have been clocked at 30 mph. (Wouldn't that be a fun job—to hang out with hippos and a stopwatch, recording their races?)

These massive animals live approximately forty-five years, and they can be extremely aggressive. So why do Joyce and Tonie Joubert have a thirteen-year-old hippopotamus named Jessica as a pet?

Jessica was only a few hours old and weighed just 351 pounds when she was found on the banks of the Blyde River, near Hoedspruit, South Africa, with her umbilical cord still attached to her. Tonie is a game ranger in the area. He and Joyce rescued her and brought her to their home, which has a walkway right to the river.

The husband and wife have left an *imprint* on Jessica. "Imprinting occurs right after birth," Joyce says. "Because my husband and I were likely the first ones she saw when her eyes opened a few hours after birth, we're the ones who have imprinted her." In other words, Jessica sees Joyce and Tonie as her parents.

Imprinting creates an extremely deep bond. And though Jessica's jaws and teeth are fiercely strong, she has never been rough with her parents. In fact, she even has house privileges! "When she enters the house, she first walks into the kitchen and puts her head on the counter. Then she eats two loaves of bread and five kilograms of carrots," Tonie says. Afterward, Jessica plops on the floor by the TV and listens to classical music. At night she sleeps outside on a mattress on the veranda with the couple's five English bull terriers.

The hippo enjoys a little more than twenty gallons of warm sweet tea every day—along with lots of grass and well-prepared sweet potatoes cut into slices. She loves it when visitors kiss her on the nose.

Jessica is tame for a few reasons—she's been loved and cared for by humans her entire life; she's around humans every day, and she doesn't have to hunt for food. But the most important factor in her becoming so tame is the imprinting. She has allowed Joyce and Tonie to define who she is. She probably believes she's human—just part of their family. God wants His children to allow Him to be their imprint. In other words, He wants to *define* you. In fact, He already has! In Isaiah 43, 44, and 45, He repeats that you're special; you've been chosen by Him and He calls you by your name. Wow!

But let's carry the defining even deeper. Will you allow the Holy Spirit to permeate your life so deeply and thoroughly that your love for God—your lifestyle, actions, and reactions—actually define who you are?

Think about it this way.

When you hear the name Michael Jordan, what immediately comes to your mind?

Or when you see Tiger Woods's name in print, what do you think of?

Just as Michael Jordan has defined basketball and Tiger Woods has defined golf, allow God to help you define Christianity in such a way that when people hear your name they automatically think of God's love. Whenever your name is seen in print, people smile and feel God's presence. Wouldn't that be awesome! Are you willing to let God imprint you?

—Susie

• •

FROM GOD:

Be imitators of God as dear children. (Ephesians 5:1 NKJV)

GO AHEAD—ANSWER:

→ Do you know someone who does a great imitation? Who is it, and what or who does that person imitate well?

→ What's the first thing that enters people's minds when they hear your name?

→ What changes would you need to make for people to think of Christ whenever they see you?

FROM SUSIE:

Can you imagine how big the scale has to be to actually weigh a hippo? Can you imagine how massive God's love is for you? So big that He actually gave His Son, Jesus Christ, to pay the death penalty for your sins! And Christ's power is so extreme that He actually conquered death. What a God!

FROM KRISTIN:

I can imitate a duck.

6.
Remember That God's Will Can't Fail

Have you ever read the book of Acts? It's the fifth book of the New Testament. It tells us about the exciting, sometimes dangerous journey of the early Christian church. It opens with Jesus ascending into heaven and continues with His 120 followers getting filled with the Holy Spirit and sharing the good news with others of what Jesus had done for them. People believed and were saved, and the church quickly grew.

Even though the Gospel spread and thousands upon thousands of people from all backgrounds began believing in Christ, things weren't easy for these early missionaries.

Often when Jesus' followers preached the Gospel, they were beaten, imprisoned, and mocked. People didn't like being told they were sinners in need of Jesus' saving grace.

If you read through to the end of the fifth chapter of Acts, Peter and a few other disciples were imprisoned (which commonly happened to those preaching the Gospel), but God sent an angel to open the jail door for them to escape. Despite the danger, they went right back to preaching about Jesus, which enraged some of the other religious leaders. Those leaders wanted them killed.

A man by the name of Gamaliel, a respected leader of the Pharisees (Pharisees were Jewish teachers and very esteemed in their culture—much like a doctor or scholar would be today), stepped up and addressed the angry crowd.

He told them not to get so upset. If the disciples weren't of God, he said, they'd fail no matter what. But if they *were* of God, nothing they did could stop the message from getting out.

Scripture doesn't say much else about Gamaliel. We don't even know if he believed in Jesus as his Savior. He reminds us of something important, though. If something is of God, no human action can stop it. This is encouraging when we're faced with extreme obstacles as we try to share the Gospel and live lives honoring to God.

Yet despite these obstacles, God's Word and the beautiful news of what Jesus did for us on the cross continues to spread. It's easy to feel like the world is hopelessly against us. Jesus charged us with an awesome mission! And the power of the Holy Spirit gives us everything we need to face trials of every kind as we seek to carry out that mission.

So don't fear the future.
If it's not of God, we *want* it to fail.
If it's of God, *nothing* on earth can stop it.

-Kristin

. . . .

FROM GOD:

Every day, in the temple and from house to house, they did not cease teaching and preaching that the Christ is Jesus. (Acts 5:42 ESV)

GO AHEAD—ANSWER:

→ Have you ever been disappointed in the outcome of something? If so, what was it?

→ What are some reasons that God might allow something to fail?

→ Does it give you comfort knowing that God has everything under control? Why?

FROM KRISTIN:

I double dare you to go read all of Acts 5 right now!

7.
Learn This Math Equation: Grace + Mercy = Forgiveness

A few years ago I heard about a church that really wanted to influence their city for Christ around Christmastime. Sure, they were inviting the public to attend their seasonal musical, and they were also serving communion at a special Christmas Eve service, but they wanted to do more. They desired to help people truly understand the concept of God's forgiveness.

They brainstormed and thought and brainstormed some more. Finally, one man shared an interesting idea. He said, "I got a parking ticket last week. It was my fault. I parked in a handicapped space, and I knew it was wrong, but I just ran into the store for less than three minutes. The parking lot was full, and I just rationalized it would be okay because I'd simply be in and out.

"But, of course, it wasn't okay. Now I have to pay the fine. If you, Pastor, would pay the fine for me, I'd never forget it!"

Everyone laughed, including the pastor. "That's pretty funny, John," he said. "But I'm not paying your ticket." Everyone continued to chuckle until John spoke again.

"But, Pastor, if you did pay my ticket, I'd never forget it. You'd be granting me grace! I'd receive unmerited favor from you for something I did that was clearly wrong."

And one by one, it began to dawn on each person in the meeting.

"That's forgiveness!" Mrs. Teeters said.

"That's mercy!" Mrs. Harrell added.

"And that's what we need to give our community," the pastor declared. "Let's go to the courthouse and get a list of unpaid traffic tickets. Then let's contact each person who owes the fine and let him know it's been paid in full!"

That's exactly what they did. They also took out a one-page ad in the local newspaper and listed the names of those who received the gift of having their fines paid and invited them to a special service at the church where they heard the pastor explain the simplicity of the Gospel: Christ loves you so very much that He willingly went to the cross and paid the death penalty you owe for your sins. All you have to do is exactly what you've done here—simply accept the gift. His gift is undeserved mercy. His gift is unmerited grace. That's forgiveness. Will you accept this gift and live for Him?

The people in that city still talk about the Christmas their fines were paid. And many are still talking about the Christmas their sins were forgiven!

—Susie

* *

FROM GOD:

God demonstrates his own love for us in this: While we were still sinners, Christ died for us. (Romans 5:8 NIV)

GO AHEAD—ANSWER:

→ Have you asked God to forgive your sins? Salvation is a free gift! Go ahead and ask Him—and then live in obedience to Him.

→ How can you keep from taking Christ's death on the cross for granted?

→ What can you do to help your non-Christian friends understand God's grace and mercy?

FROM SUSIE

There's no better gift in the world than God's forgiveness.

8.
Double-Check Your Motives

Have you ever done something nice for someone, hoping that in return they'd do something nice for you later on down the road? Then when they didn't do what you'd hoped, you got a little upset with them? After all, *you* helped *them* out!

It's nice when we can help each other out, but it's not fair to attach unspoken strings to a favor or act of kindness. We can't get upset with someone for not doing something they didn't know they were supposed to do. If we're doing something only so that we can turn it around for a favor later, it proves our motives are wrong.

Sometimes we do the same thing with God. We obey and do good things, hoping that God will notice and in return give us what we want.

We try and earn God's favor. Except we cannot earn something that's free. We don't do good things because of what we'll get but because of what we've already received.

Doing things for the wrong reason leads to bitterness, envy, and anger toward God when He doesn't give us what we think we're owed. (Often they're things He never promised us. God *always* delivers on things He promises.)

God doesn't change—and neither does His love for us. We give, help, show compassion, love, and sacrifice because of what He's already given, not because of what we hope will be given.

God gave *everything* for us when He sent Jesus to die on the cross. We've already been given forgiveness of our sins, right standing with God, and the promise of eternal life. Even if nothing good ever happened to us the rest of our lives, that would still be enough.

-Kristin

FROM GOD:

> He said also to the man who had invited him, "When you give a dinner or a banquet, do not invite your friends or your brothers or your relatives or rich neighbors, lest they also invite you in return and you be repaid. But when you give a feast, invite the poor, the crippled, the lame, the blind, and you will be blessed, because they cannot repay you. For you will be repaid at the resurrection of the just." (Luke 14:12–14 ESV)

GO AHEAD—ANSWER:

→ When was a time your motives were in the wrong place?

→ Do you feel as though God loves you more when good things are happening? Why?

→ Do you feel God owes you something? If yes, what and why?

FROM KRISTIN:

We often focus on what we want to get instead of what we've already been given. Don't forget to thank God for all He's done for you. Most importantly, thank Him for the greatest gift of all: Jesus.

9.
Stop Lying

Do you remember the children's fairy tale about Pinocchio? The story says that he was created by a wood-carver named Geppetto in a small Italian village. Geppetto created him as a wooden puppet, but Pinocchio dreamed of becoming a real boy.

The event that most people remember about this popular children's story is that Pinocchio's nose grew in length each time he told a lie. At one point in the story, his nose grew so long a bird built a nest on it!

What if this could really happen? Can you imagine people walking around with noses as long as their body is tall? I'm five feet two inches tall. What if my nose were six feet long? I wouldn't be able to walk! It would be impossible for my body to balance itself.

Or what if it weren't our noses that grew during lies? What if it were our ears? Can you imagine someone with twenty-pound ears? Or what if it were our thumbs? It's ridiculous, isn't it!

But it's just as ridiculous to lie. To bend the truth. To deceive someone.

A lot of people don't think twice about lying. Even though that's pathetic, it's also expected behavior of those who don't know Christ. But what's really shocking is when Christians lie! Or maybe I should say, what's really shocking is *when people who call themselves Christians* lie.

Did you know that lying actually breaks one of the Ten Commandments? (See Exodus 10:1–6 for all of the Ten Commandments; see Exodus 20:16 for the command not to lie.) It's a big deal to break one of the Ten Commandments. It's a sin! It's a sin to lie.

Do you find yourself casually lying to those around you? It's an easy habit to get into; it's a difficult habit to break. Often liars have to create other lies to cover up for the first lies, and then they have to create even more lies to cover up the later lies. Lying quickly becomes a vicious cycle. Like a tornado, it can become extremely damaging to you and to those around you.

Strive to become a young woman of integrity who can be trusted, who is dependable and honest.

Choose your words carefully, and determine to live a life of honesty.

—Susie

• •

FROM GOD:

The LORD detests lying lips, but he delights in people who are trustworthy. (Proverbs 12:22 NIV)

GO AHEAD—ANSWER:

→ Are there certain areas of your life (curfew, accomplishments, grades, etc.) in which you tend to bend the truth?

→ Are there specific people to whom you're most tempted to lie?

→ If you've been lying, have you asked God to forgive you? He will. Then ask Him to help you to live a life of honesty and to give you the strength to break the cycle of lying.

FROM SUSIE:

Kristin has seven toes on her right foot.

FROM KRISTIN:

I do not! You're lying.

FROM SUSIE:

No, I was kidding. But sometimes there's a fine line between lying and kidding. Maybe we need to write a devotional on that.

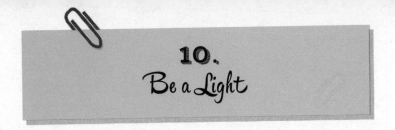

10.
Be a Light

Have you ever tried growing a garden in the dark? I'll give you a little spoiler on how this garden will turn out: not very good. Nothing's going to grow into a fully mature plant without a little bit of light.

Have you ever overturned a rock and watched as the bugs underneath scattered around, trying to escape the light and get back to the comfort of the dark?

Have you ever been reading in a room at dusk and didn't realize it was getting dark until someone flicked on the lights and asked, "Is that better?"

Light is powerful.

It helps us see things clearly. It sends darkness running. It nourishes and strengthens. Light brings hope, growth, and life.

Plants can't generate light on their own. They have to get it from an outside source.

Just as plants can't generate light on their own, neither can we. Our light must also come from somewhere else.

In the book of Matthew, Jesus tells us that we (Christians) are the light of the world. We get this light, though, because Jesus dwells in us. Wherever we go, we shine His light, helping to expose the darkness of sin and bringing hope and life.

We must keep this flame burning. Through meditating on His Word, praying, and learning more about God, we're nourished and grow as believers. Our light shines brighter and brighter until it can't help but overflow and pour out into the world.

–Kristin

• •

FROM GOD:

The light shines in the darkness, and the darkness has not overcome it. (John 1:5 ESV)

GO AHEAD—ANSWER:

→ Have you ever been afraid of the dark?

→ What's the best way to get rid of the darkness? (It's not a trick question.)

→ As a Christian, how can you specifically be God's light in the dark world we live in?

FROM KRISTIN:

I once had a lava lamp. It was the *best* light until it fell and broke and the "lava" exploded all over my room. Then I needed to find another light to clean up my other light. The lava lamp is like if you fall down, and. . . Never mind. That analogy is a stretch. Just stay in the Word and don't drop your lava lamp.

FROM SUSIE:

I once had a rabbit.

11.
Keep Your Anger on a Tight Leash

I can't help but notice how common it's becoming for professional coaches to yell at the officials. They get right in each other's faces! And pro athletes often yell at their opponents. I see their nostrils flare, their veins popping out on their necks, and I hear their volume steadily rise to a frightening level.

What's the deal?

Why are so many pro athletes—and even coaches—being slapped with astronomical fines and getting kicked out of games and arenas because of their tempers? It's because anger is a dangerous emotion.

Think about it. Anger is usually at the root of murder, jealousy, physical assault, and many other crimes. Anger hurts! It hurts the person who's angry, and it also hurts the recipient.

Does that mean we should never get angry? No. We wouldn't be human if we didn't sometimes feel and express anger. Even Jesus got angry. But we *do* need to be extremely selective in what we choose to become angry about, and we should think twice about how we express our anger.

If you express your anger by putting your fist through a wall, something is wrong. If you show your anger by hitting someone, you're out of control. If you express your anger by yelling at your parents, you're going to be in trouble.

There are acceptable ways of expressing anger. Try writing in your journal. Or jog around the block a few times. Hit tennis balls against a backboard for thirty minutes. Breathe deeply until you feel more in control. Always pray when you're angry!

Do the things that anger you really *need* to anger you? If you're angry because tater tots aren't being served in the school cafeteria today, you're letting your emotions have too much control. If you're angry because you're studying human trafficking and have realized how horrific it is, your anger is justified.

Jesus didn't portray frivolous anger. When He was angry, He had a good reason. When He knocked the tables over in the temple and chased out the money changers, He displayed proper anger—not the selfish anger we often exhibit. He did this because the money changers were taking advantage of innocent people.

See, Judea was under the rule of the Romans, and the money currently being used was Roman money. The Jewish law required that every man pay a tribute to the service of the sanctuary of "half a shekel" (see Exodus 30:11–16). But the shekel was a Jewish coin. So to make things convenient, the law allowed money changers to set up tables in the temple so people could exchange their Jewish coins for Roman money and then pay the amount they owed.

The problem? The money changers got greedy and started charging to exchange the money. Because thousands of people needed to have their money changed, this became a highly profitable business inside the temple.

Jesus immediately recognized the greed and profit flowing throughout the temple, and He became angry because the temple was supposed to be a place of worship and pure devotion to God.

He wasn't against the exchange of money. He was against what the temple had become—a place of greed and profit for a few individuals. He cleansed the temple to restore it to what God intended it to be.

Jesus displayed what is known as *righteous anger.* To be angry about things that are evil is always acceptable. But again, we need to be careful about how we express that anger and to whom we express it. Jesus expressed His anger toward the right people—those who were guilty.

If you express your anger about human trafficking by screaming at your best friend, your anger is misplaced. If you could scream at those who kidnap innocent children and sell them into slavery, you'd be properly expressing your anger at the right people. (But that would be dangerous, and you might be killed. So try writing your elected representatives at the state and national levels or talking with your pastor about getting a group together in your church to get involved with an organization that works to stop human trafficking.)

You can get angry, but get angry for the right reasons and express your anger effectively.

—Susie

FROM GOD:

A hot-tempered person stirs up conflict, but the one who is patient calms a quarrel. (Proverbs 15:18 NIV)

GO AHEAD—ANSWER:

→ What tends to make you angry?

→ How do you most often express your anger?

→ Will you ask God to help you refrain from getting so angry? Also ask Him to teach you to express righteous anger in the right way.

FROM SUSIE:

Human trafficking is a serious matter, and it's one that truly makes Kristin and me extremely angry. Christian persecution is another thing we both take seriously. What are some things that you take very seriously? Have you discovered ways to get involved?

FROM KRISTIN:

Bad anger makes you drive your fist through a wall. Good anger drives you to help make positive change.

12.
Remember What Christ Has Done for You

The spotted hyena is the largest of the three hyena species. They're known as scavengers and often eat the leftovers that other animals leave behind. But they can also be predators and have one of the strongest sets of jaws in the entire animal kingdom. Their teeth are so formidable, they can even bite through the bones of their prey! These ugly animals' high-pitched squeals often sound like hideous laughter.

A spotted hyena usually weighs around a hundred pounds and can run at approximately 35 mph. Kevin Richardson lives in South Africa and has worked his way inside a sophisticated hierarchy of dangerous spotted hyenas by doing things the animal way.

"I've worked with large predators most of my life," he says. "But a few years ago, I established a place to study the habits of the spotted hyena." He developed a passion for the animal and wanted to learn all he could about this dangerous yet interesting species.

The spotted hyena is actually a highly intelligent animal with keen senses of seeing and hearing. Built for power, it kills small prey by crushing the skull with its jaws.

Kevin has been hospitalized five times due to hyena bites and attacks. "They can be extremely aggressive animals," he says. "But a hyena in captivity can be very tame."

The clan of spotted hyenas that Kevin has been working with aren't tame. They're wild animals, yet he has eventually worked his way inside the clan. He's been slowly earning their trust for the past fourteen years. "They now treat me as one of their own," he says. "They're finally seeing me as simply another hyena."

Kevin plays with them, rubs their tummies, and wrestles with them. "They no longer see me as a threat. They know my smell; they recognize me." (See "Growing Up: Hyena" on YouTube.)

He definitely has an extraordinary relationship with these animals and says that each one even has a distinct, individual personality.

ooooo

Does the above story seem a bit outrageous? Maybe it seems a little far-fetched. Some people would find it hard to believe that Kevin has actually been welcomed into a cackle of hyenas! It's difficult to take this true story for granted.

But shouldn't it also be amazing to realize that Christ was willing to leave the perfection of heaven to be born in a filthy cave, live in a sinful world, and die for our sins simply because He loves us so much and wants us to live with Him forever?

Yes! What Christ has done for us is the most amazing thing we'll ever encounter. Yet we often take His love, His death, and His forgiveness for granted. We hear about a man living with hyenas and tend to say, "Wow! That's amazing!" But we often react to the good news of the Gospel as less than exciting.

Why is this? Could it be that we haven't fully realized the magnitude of what Christ has done for us? Undeserving as we are, He declares us not guilty if we'll simply confess our sins, accept His forgiveness, and live for Him. Wow! That's amazing!

—Susie

• •

FROM GOD:

If we confess our sins, he is faithful and just to forgive us our sins, and to cleanse us from all unrighteousness. (1 John 1:9 KJV)

GO AHEAD—ANSWER:

→ Describe something you view as truly amazing.

→ Describe what you imagine it's like to be crucified on a splinter-filled cross, after having the skin on your back barely attached due to being whipped, and being so tortured that you hardly appear human.

→ Why do many Christians hardly think twice about all Christ has done for us? Spend time thanking Him this week for all He has done and is currently doing for *you*.

FROM SUSIE:

Kevin had to work his way into acceptance by spotted hyenas. I'm extremely grateful that I don't have to work my way into Christ's acceptance! He loves me more than I can comprehend, and I can't wait to spend eternity with Him in heaven.

FROM KRISTIN:

I'm just really glad I don't have spots, unless freckles count as spots.

13.
Be Slap Happy

Back in the olden days—well, 1988—Bobby McFerrin released a song titled "Don't Worry, Be Happy." It became the first a cappella song to reach number one on the *Billboard* Hot 100 chart, and it stayed number one for two weeks.

The song is often used in TV and movies to accompany light-hearted scenes. You may have heard it in the movies *Flushed Away*, *Wall-E*, *Jarhead*, or *Dawn of the Dead.* Or perhaps you heard it on one of these TV shows: *That '70s Show*, *Futurama*, *Nip/Tuck*, *The Fresh Prince of Bel-Air*, or *The Simpsons.*

Google the lyrics to the song. (Go ahead, I'll wait right here.)

There are lots and lots of "ooh, ooh, ooh, ooh oo-oohs."

There's not a lot to the song, but it sure has seen a lot of success! And I'm wondering if it's because deep down people really want happiness. The song carries a happy-go-lucky tune that makes listeners want to snap their fingers, whistle, and just lay back and take life easy. It's almost irresistible.

But I'm also wondering if happiness is overrated. Don't get me wrong—I want to be happy. But our *real* purpose in life isn't simply to be happy; it's to glorify God in all we do. Too often we lose sight of this! It's easy to concentrate on our happiness, but when we do that, it causes us to look inward instead of upward toward God.

He desires that we focus our attention on Him—not ourselves. I can almost hear your thoughts: *But, Susie! Surely God wants us to be happy.*

Well, He wants us to be *joyful*. In fact, joy is one of the fruits of the Holy Spirit (see Galatians 5:22–23). Maybe we should take a peek at the definitions, because joy and happiness are really two different things.

The dictionary defines *happiness* as a "state of well-being, a pleasurable or satisfying experience." The definition of the word *rejoice* from which we get the word *joy* is "to be glad; take delight" (see dictionary.reference.com). Get this: the Bible uses the words *happy* and *happiness* about thirty times. But the words *joy* and *rejoice* are used more than three hundred times! According to James

1:2, we can have a deep, genuine joy as we abide in Christ, even in the midst of trials. We may not feel happy about battling trials, but we can experience genuine joy knowing we're in the center of God's will. Joy goes much deeper than happiness. Happiness is fleeting; joy is everlasting.

Could it be that God is way more interested in putting aside your temporary happiness to develop your character and establish joy in your life? Many people get divorced today simply because, as they say, "I'm just not happy anymore."

Flash forward a few years and place yourself in the above situation. Think about this: What if God wants you to find fulfillment in an intimate, growing relationship with Him in spite of the fact that you may be in a less-than-ideal marriage? Would you allow Him to develop true joy in your life in spite of that?

Let's say you find out tomorrow that you have cancer. Obviously, you're not going to be happy about that! But what if God wants to develop an inner joy in your soul as you quietly trust Him in the midst of a terminal illness? Will you allow Him to do so?

Perhaps we've gotten sidetracked with being happy. Remember, our goal in living is to glorify our Maker. And in doing so, joy becomes the automatic result.

—Susie

• •

FROM GOD:

May the God of hope fill you with all joy and peace as you trust in him, so that you may overflow with hope by the power of the Holy Spirit. (Romans 15:13 NIV)

GO AHEAD—ANSWER:

→ Describe a time when you've been happy and a time when you've experienced genuine joy. What was the difference?

→ How does putting so much emphasis on happiness make it all about us?

→ Describe a time when you experienced joy in spite of battling tough times.

FROM SUSIE:

I'm not happy about the fact that Applebee's restaurants don't serve Coca-Cola. But I'm joyful when I'm there eating a salad, talking about Jesus, and sharing prayer requests with my friend Jan.

FROM KRISTIN:

I'm not happy that you and Jan went to Applebee's without me.

14.
Learn to Deal with Mean Girls

At some point you've probably interacted with a mean girl. Mean girls intentionally tear others down to bring themselves up. They mock, disrespect, exclude, and make other people's lives miserable because it gives them a sense of superiority.

Dealing with mean girls became even more complicated with the onset of social media. You no longer get to leave the cruel, hurtful remarks at school. They follow you home on Twitter, Instagram, and Facebook. (Wait, do you guys still use Facebook?)

Unfortunately, it's nearly impossible to avoid mean girls entirely. There are, however, some measures you can take to limit the amount of power they have over your life.

1. *Don't hang around them any more than necessary.* You're probably around mean girls because they're in your class at school or extracurricular activity. Don't go out of your way to be their best friend, and don't try to work your way into their good graces. Be kind and friendly when you're around them, but don't make them your closest buddies.

2. *View this as an opportunity to grow thick skin.* Throughout life you're going to encounter mean people. One time a woman yelled loudly and inappropriately at me in a restaurant for pointing out that she was next in line to order. The employee at the empty register tried calling and waving the woman over multiple times. Assuming she didn't see or hear the employee, I said, "Excuse me, ma'am. I think the register there is open." She proceeded to call me all sorts of foul names at the top of her lungs—which made all the restaurant patrons turn their heads and stare at us. I ran through my actions in my head. Had I been rude? Impatient? Out of line? No. She was cranky and probably having a bad day (or month, or year, or life). If I'd taken her outburst personally, it would have ruined my day also.

3. *If things get out of control, talk to your parents, teacher, or other person in charge and ask if there's a way you can be in a*

different class or group. It's not always possible to get away, but it doesn't hurt to try.

4. *Keep all your social media private, and don't let the mean girls follow you.* You're not obligated to let everyone follow you online. If people only want to follow you to make fun of you, it's wise not to give them that power—even if it means having a few less followers.

5. *Pray for them.* Crazy, right? It's hard to have any compassion or mercy on someone whose sole purpose seems to be making your life miserable. It's easier to fantasize about how you'll get even or make them wish they'd been nicer. You may want to retaliate and seek revenge, or at least watch them fall. But we're called to love and pray for those who torment us.

   Mean girls are often that way because they're insecure or going through trials at home, or because being mean gives them a sense of power. (Susie will go into more detail on the importance of praying for bullies in a couple of chapters.)

6. *Be an example.* You can't control other people's behavior, but you can control your own. You can be a beacon of light and a breath of fresh air to those around you. You can show the world that being mean isn't necessary for living a happy, full life.

-Kristin

• •

FROM GOD:

"So whatever you wish that others would do to you, do also to them, for this is the Law and the Prophets." (Matthew 7:12 ESV)

GO AHEAD—ANSWER:

→ Have you dealt with mean girls? What happened?

→ Why do you think mean girls act that way?

→ How can we, as Christians, be an example to mean girls?

FROM KRISTIN:

Don't take for granted the friends around you who treat people kindly and love you for you.

FROM SUSIE:

I'm yelling loudly because you didn't take me with you to the restaurant.

15.
Don't Be a Mean Girl

Now that we've talked about dealing with mean girls, take a moment and evaluate your own behavior.

Are you catty to other girls?

Do you intentionally find and point out flaws in your friends in a way that's destructive?

Do you constantly talk bad about your friends and people you don't like when they're not around?

Do you make jokes at the expense of others around you?

Do you feel like you're above authority? Do you disrespect, disobey, and insult your teachers, parents, and leaders?

Do your friends seem to be intimidated by you or even afraid of you?

If this sounds like you, you might be a mean girl.

If you read the above and felt convicted, that's good news! Feeling sorrow for a way you've acted means you're willing to repent and change. (Mean girls, wanting to stay mean, generally don't read spiritual advice books or feel bad about their behavior.)

As a teenager, I discovered I could make people laugh. Unfortunately, I often did it by putting down those around me. Even though everyone around me laughed, the person I'd put down felt terrible. At one point someone pulled me aside and told me that my words were hurting people. I realized I was being mean and needed to change. I became more conscious of the power my words had and tried to use them to uplift instead of tear down.

I discovered it was much more fun to make jokes everyone could enjoy! And I didn't know it at the time, but God was giving me practice for when I became a comedian. To this day I try to be conscious of my jokes and keep them from being mean spirited.

Mean-girl syndrome makes you feel good at the time. It gives you a sense of superiority and control. It's short lived, however. Mean girls are passive-aggressive bullies and eventually get their comeuppance.

–Kristin

FROM GOD:

The words of the reckless pierce like swords, but the tongue of the wise brings healing. (Proverbs 12:18 NIV)

GO AHEAD—ANSWER!

→ Do you act like a mean girl? Be honest.

→ Why do you think it's easy to sometimes slip into "mean girl" behavior?

→ Ask God to make you aware of any "mean girl" behavior.

FROM KRISTIN:

If you've been a mean girl, apologize to those who took the brunt of your meanness. A sincere apology goes a long way in repairing relationships.

16.
Pray for the Bullies

Sixteen-year-old Allie told me she's waiting until marriage to have sex. "That's great," I affirmed.

"Yeah, but it's like I'm wearing a target around my neck," she said.

"What do you mean?"

"Well, because I'm a virgin, I get bullied a lot. In the locker room after volleyball practice, the girls on the team brag about who they're sleeping with. When the conversation turns to me, I tell them that I'm waiting until marriage. And they not only laugh and make fun of me, but they post stuff on Facebook and spread all kinds of stupid rumors about me."

"Like what?"

"They say I'm gay or I'm an ice queen or any number of things. I hate it. It really hurts."

"I'm sure it does. But on your wedding night, you'll be able to give your husband a gift that none of these girls will be able to give their future husbands. And at that time, it will definitely be worth the bullying you're experiencing now."

"I know that's true. But it doesn't make it any easier right now."

"Here's an idea: let's start praying for the girls who are bullying you."

"Susie, that's crazy!"

"I know it sounds crazy, but let's see if it will make a difference."

Do you know *your* prayers make a difference? The awesome thing about prayer is that God answers every single prayer you pray! You don't always get the answer when you want it, and He doesn't always answer the way you want Him to, but He always answers prayer!

Knowing that's true, it just makes sense to pray for those who are hurting you. Did you know that it's hard to be angry at someone for whom you're praying?

Years ago I attended a church that hired a new staff member. He was gruff, impersonal, and impatient with people. I really didn't like this guy. It was hard for me to even smile at him when I saw him at church. Yet I knew God wanted me to love him.

It was hard, but I began praying for him. I asked God to help me see him through His eyes and not my own. I determined to look beyond his actions and try to see his heart—his motives. And during the year, I felt my heart begin to soften. I realized that he really did care about people; he just didn't always know how to show it. By the end of the year, I actually began liking him and his family.

They moved away a few years later, but I saw them again. And when we caught up with each other, I actually enjoyed spending time with him. God had changed him—and He had also changed me!

Sometimes God may choose not to change the other person, but He can always change you. Jesus prayed for His enemies, and He told His disciples to do the same. We'll never come out on top by yelling back at a bully. But God can do the impossible: He can soften a bully's heart, and He can change your perspective.

—Susie

. . . .

FROM GOD:

"Bless those who curse you, pray for those who mistreat you." (Luke 6:28 NIV)

GO AHEAD—ANSWER:

→ Have you been bullied? If so, describe the situation.

→ How did you handle being bullied?

→ Have you ever bullied another person?

FROM SUSIE:

Bullying doesn't always come in demonstrative actions. Sometimes we bully people by intimidating them, ignoring them, making them feel guilty about something, or manipulating them. Make it your goal to have no part of being a bully. Instead, notice who they are and pray for them.

17.
Stop Biting, Picking at, or Chewing Your Nails

I'm not a nail biter. I'm pretty germ conscious, and the thought of sticking my hands in my mouth grosses me out. (When you spend a lot of time in airports, you become hyperaware of disease.)

I am, however, a nail "picker." I pick, peel, and tear at my nails when I'm bored, antsy, anxious, or worried. As a result, my nails are rough little stubs. A couple of times I picked at them so much they got raw and bled.

I decided recently it was time to kick this bad habit to the curb. While I occasionally still have to remind myself to stop picking, a few things helped me break the habit. If you're a nail biter or picker, maybe these will help you.

1. Keep nail clippers handy. I have to keep my nails short because I play several instruments. If I'm able to clip them as needed, I'm less tempted to pick.

2. I'm naturally fidgety, so I try and keep something around to play with. I'll crochet or knit if I'm sitting around the house, or I'll stick my hands in my pockets and play with a piece of string or a coin. (It's a little goofy but effective.)

3. Ask a few people to remind you to stop if they see you reverting to your old habit.

4. Paint your nails. The nail polish will make you more aware of your hands and what they're doing.

5. My nail-biting friends have told me they put nasty-tasting polish on them to deter biting. This didn't help me personally as a picker, but it's worth considering if you're a nail biter.

6. Keep your hands well manicured to give you incentive to keep them beautiful.

7. Come up with a fun reward to help get you motivated! Better yet, pick a reward that involves your family and friends

(e.g., pizza party, zoo outing, movie) and make it a community effort!

-Kristin

• •

FROM GOD:

"All things are lawful for me," but not all things are helpful. "All things are lawful for me," but I will not be dominated by anything. (1 Corinthians 6:12 ESV)

GO AHEAD—ANSWER:

→ Are you a nail biter or picker?

→ Have you tried breaking a bad habit before? How did it go?

→ What are some other ways you can think of to get rid of bad habits?

FROM KRISTIN:

It takes twenty-one days to break a bad habit and establish a new one. So get a calendar and put a sticker on each day you successfully go without biting or picking at your nails!

FROM SUSIE:

I'm just really glad you don't pick your nose.

FROM KRISTIN:
Well. . .

18.
Send Something through the Postal System

Ripley's Believe It or Not! hosts an annual Strange Mail Contest. And it really is strange! Participants can't package anything inside a box, wrapper, or envelope. The postage and address have to be placed directly on the item being mailed.

The winning item in 2014 was a tree trunk with a horseshoe embedded in it. I guess you can send just about anything in the mail—unless it's dangerous. So I tried it. I sent Kristin a smiley-face-emoji pillow. I didn't put it inside a box or anything. I just taped her name and address on it, took it to the post office, stamped it, and mailed it. Guess what! She got it three days later.

John lost his job. . .and then lost his initiative to find a new one. He began watching so much TV that a relative sent him a potato through the mail with his name and address written on one side of the potato and this message on the other side: "Get off the couch!" That's a pretty creative way of communicating with a couch potato.

Instead of sending a postcard from her vacation in Hawaii, Mallory grabbed a Sharpie and wrote the name and address of her mom on a coconut and mailed that instead. Her mom loved it—and ate the coconut!

Amy was bummed that her BFF couldn't spend spring break with her in Cancún. While she was sunbathing on the beach one morning, she kicked off her flip-flops, addressed one to her friend, wrote "Wishing you were here" on it, and sent it through the mail. Yes, it arrived safely.

Mark and his college roommate loved playing Frisbee golf. After graduation, Mark moved away, got married, and began his career. But he never forgot his fun days of Frisbee golf. So he bought a Frisbee, wrote his former roommate's name and address on it, stamped it, and mailed it. What a great way to remind someone of fun memories!

What can *you* send someone? Well. . .just about anything, as long as it's properly addressed with a permanent marker. Here are a few ideas:

- Mail a brick to someone who's been a solid foundation in your life.

- Host a summer barbecue and mail plastic pigs to your friends. Address one side of the pig and write the invitation information on the other.

- Grab an orange and write, "Orange you glad you have a crazy friend like me?" and mail it to a friend.

- Do you have a friend who moved away? Find an old bed pillow you're not using anymore, and write her name and address on the right half of the pillow. On the left half write, "Hey, girlfriend! Here's a big hug from me to you. I miss you."

Of course, you don't have to send something weird or wacky through the mail to remind someone you're thinking of them. People simply love getting something in the mail. So make time to send a letter, a note, or a card—anything that will brighten someone's day.

—Susie

FROM GOD:

A joyful heart is good medicine. (Proverbs 17:22 ESV)

GO AHEAD—ANSWER:

→ What's the coolest thing you've ever received in the mail?

→ What's the most special thing you've ever mailed to someone?

→ Will you mail someone something special this week?

FROM SUSIE:

I'm thinking about mailing the neighbor's cat to Kristin.

FROM KRISTIN:

I'm mailing you my neighbor's camel. Yes, my neighbors actually raise camels.

19.
Practice Love

I've attended many weddings, and very often the pastor officiating the wedding reads a part of the Bible called the "Love Chapter." It goes like this: "Love is patient and kind; love does not envy or boast; it is not arrogant or rude. It does not insist on its own way; it is not irritable or resentful; it does not rejoice at wrongdoing, but rejoices with the truth. Love bears all things, believes all things, hopes all things, endures all things" (1 Corinthians 13:4–7 ESV).

On paper love sounds pretty easy, right? Movies and television make love look simple, magical, and obvious.

Love is beautifully simple in theory: put the other person ahead of yourself.

In real life, however, pride, emotions, anger, laziness, and self-ishness all get in the way of our ability to love.

Have you ever watched a runner glide over hurdles or a gymnast dismount the bars precisely and perfectly? They make something difficult look incredibly easy because they've practiced, trained, and sacrificed to accomplish a skill.

Love is no different. It takes practice, commitment, and discipline.

When you want to yell at your parents for making you do something that seems unfair, practice love by speaking gently and obeying.

When you want to retaliate at your sister for constantly taking your things without asking, practice love by showing patience and talking to her calmly about your annoyances.

When you make the volleyball team and your best friend doesn't, practice love by not boasting or rubbing your success in her face.

Love is difficult, and we'll fail often. Like athletes, however, we need to pick ourselves up and continue training. Remember, God didn't leave us helpless in our ability to love. We're able to love others because Jesus set the example by loving us perfectly.

–Kristin

FROM GOD:

"A new commandment I give to you, that you love one another: just as I have loved you, you also are to love one another. By this all people will know that you are my disciples, if you have love for one another." (John 13:34–35 ESV)

GO AHEAD—ANSWER:

→ Why is love so difficult?

→ Why does God call us to love one another?

→ What are some ways you can practice love?

FROM KRISTIN:

Roses, chocolates, and candlelight dinners are culture's idea of true love. True, *true* love, however, is getting up at 5:00 a.m. to drive someone an hour to the airport. (Stopping for doughnuts on the way, of course.)

FROM SUSIE:

Speaking of. . . Can I get a ride to the airport?

FROM KRISTIN:

You live ten hours away from me!

FROM SUSIE:

I'll buy you an entire box of doughnuts.

FROM KRISTIN:
Done.

20.
Start a Spiritual Journal

Maybe you've had an English teacher who required you to keep a journal. If so, you can relate to my former creative writing students. But I tried to make journal writing fun by giving them a variety of assignments.

For example, one day I asked them to fill a page by listing as many blue things as they could think of. Another day: Draw a picture of your favorite room in your house—using the hand you don't normally write with. Another assignment? Write "Journaling Is Totally Cool" at the top of the page and then find as many words as possible out of those four words.

On another day they simply filled the page with questions. One journal assignment was to create the worst possible food combinations they could list to fill the page. (Some examples: corn dog cooked in vinegar, an Oreo saturated in mustard, 7UP mixed with sour milk.)

Most of the time when we think about journaling, we assume it means we simply write about our day. But journaling can be as creative as you can make it. And spiritual journaling is even better because it centers around your relationship with Christ. So grab a notebook, and let's get started.

Day 1: Write your testimony. This is simply your personal story of how you became a Christian. Keep it short, and write it in three parts: Before, How, and After. (If you're not a believer yet, write where you are in your spiritual journey. What questions do you have? What are you learning?) In the Before part, describe in one paragraph what your life was like before you asked Christ to forgive your sins and live in your heart. (Maybe you were selfish, self-centered, into drugs and alcohol. Perhaps you were deceitful or you cheated, stole, or had anger issues.)

Now let's move to the How area. Write a paragraph about how you met Christ. (Was it at church, camp, a Christian concert, or through reading your Bible?)

And for your final paragraph, describe the difference Christ has made—and is still making—in your life after you committed yourself to Him.

Day 2: Write down the names of your family members. Beside each name list something you want to pray about for that person. Example: Maybe your brother needs a job, your sister is concerned about the math test she's taking today, and your mom needs encouragement. If you don't know specifically what they *need*, then simply list a blessing you'd like for them to experience: peace, help, guidance, and so on. Don't forget to write your own name and list **your** prayer requests as well!

Day 3: Cut pictures out of magazines, or take photos with your phone, print them out, and glue them onto pages in your journal. The catch? Every photo must reflect the majesty of God.

Day 4: Write Blessings at the top of your page. Now list all the blessings you can come up with that God has given you.

Day 5: List the names of your friends and extended family members. Beside each name list something you want to pray about for that person.

Day 6: Look up Psalm 1 in your Bible. Copy it inside your journal. Then rewrite it in your own words.

Day 7: Go back through your prayer requests and list any answers to prayer you have received this week. Underneath your answers, write a prayer of gratitude to God. If you haven't yet experienced the answers, write a prayer telling God you trust His perfect timing.

—Susie

. . . .

FROM GOD:

> But grow in the grace and knowledge of our Lord and Savior Jesus Christ. (2 Peter 3:18 NIV)

GO AHEAD—ANSWER:

→ Have you ever kept a journal? What were the advantages?

→ How can keeping a spiritual journal enhance your relationship with Christ?

→ Will you begin a spiritual journal today? Ask a friend to start one with you!

FROM SUSIE:

Today, Father, I'm thanking You for Kristin's friendship. Surprise her today with a special blessing.

FROM KRISTIN:

Today I received a smiley face pillow in the mail!

21.
Continue Your Spiritual Journal

As you continue your spiritual journal, you'll grow closer to Christ and will begin to realize the power of prayer. We're going to incorporate reading the Bible into our spiritual journal this week.

Day 8: Read the first chapter of the Gospel of John. Before you begin reading, ask God to speak to you through His Word. As you move through the first chapter, stop after a few verses and list in your journal something that stands out to you. Keep reading, stop, and list something else. Do this throughout the entire chapter.

Example: After I read the first five verses, I stopped and wrote, "No darkness—no matter *how* dark—can ever hide the light of God. Even the smallest trace of God's light can't be hidden by darkness. Yay!"

Day 9: Write a paragraph about what you'd like God to teach you. Then go back to Day 2 and pray for each of your family members by name.

Day 10: Read John 2. List any questions you have about what you read. Also, write out something to praise God for in what you read.

Day 11: Write GOD'S MERCIES ARE EVERLASTING at the top of your page. Now find as many words as you can create out of those four words and list them in your journal. Ask God to help you become all He wants you to be.

Day 12: Read John 3. What is God saying to you through His Word? Write about it. Then turn back to Day 5 and pray for every person on your list.

Day 13: Ask God to show you how He was reflected in your life today, and write that down. For example, you felt His nudge to clean the house for your mom without being asked, or you sensed He was leading you to smile at a stranger, or you allowed someone to go in front of you in the checkout line.

Now ask God to reveal to you the areas of today that He wants to help you improve. For instance, maybe you were sassy with a parent, or perhaps you were deceitful about something or insisted on having your own way. Go back through your day and list how you could have changed your actions in each specific situation to honor God.

Day 14: Have you experienced any answers to prayer? List them. Also, write a thank-you note to God for helping you grow closer to Him.

As you continue journaling, repeat this pattern—and feel free to add to this outline. But continue to read the Bible consistently and to pray daily! These are the key elements in your spiritual journal.

—Susie

• •

FROM GOD:

Live a life worthy of the Lord and please him in every way: bearing fruit in every good work, growing in the knowledge of God. (Colossians 1:10 NIV)

GO AHEAD—ANSWER:

→ In what specific way would you like to grow spiritually (more faith, wisdom, discernment, boldness, etc.)?

→ How can you develop the above areas in your life?

→ Are you willing to increase your Bible reading and your prayer life?

FROM SUSIE:

We're kidding ourselves if we think we can grow closer to Christ without reading the Bible and praying. Those are the key ingredients to spiritual strength and intimacy with Him.

22.
Persist, Persist, Persist

Life gets tough sometimes, and it's tempting to give up. We want to give up on being kind and give in to our anger. We want to quit school, a job, a team, or even our family or our faith. We just want out.

Persistence requires a certain mind-set—a determination to work toward a goal and adjust as obstacles come up.

Some goals, like "graduate high school" or "run a marathon," have a definite finish line. Other goals, such as "grow in the Lord" or "be kind to people," require determination until you die. These goals are harder to measure, but the rewards are eternal.

Faith and character goals require persistence. Even when (actually, *especially* when) you're overwhelmed, stressed, and tired, lean on God and persist. Recognize your tendency to lash out and sin in these situations. Respond with prayer and by seeking out good friends and family who can encourage you and remind you that this pain or discomfort is temporary (even if it has no ending in sight).

We're to persist toward the ultimate goal: the calling of Jesus Christ (Philippians 3:14). When we get to heaven, we'll get our reward and hear the sweet, sweet words spoken to us by our Father, "Well done, good and faithful servant" (Matthew 25:21 ESV).

–Kristin

. . . .

FROM GOD:

Let us not grow weary of doing good, for in due season we will reap, if we do not give up. (Galatians 6:9 ESV)

GO AHEAD—ANSWER:

→ What is persistence?

→ What are some areas where you've persisted well?

→ What are some areas where you need more persistence?

FROM KRISTIN:

I'm happy to say that despite many obstacles (craving Chipotle counts as an obstacle, right?) I persisted and finished this chapter!

FROM SUSIE:

I don't think Mexican food is ever an obstacle. It's a blessing, Kristin. A b-l-e-s-s-i-n-g! In fact, I think I'll go get blessed right now.

23.
Clean the Bathtub

I'll never forget it. I was in the fourth grade and my friend Hannah spent the night at my house. (Hannah isn't her real name. I changed it in case she reads this. I would never want her to be embarrassed.) It was Saturday night, and we took turns taking our baths for Sunday morning the evening before.

I bathed, cleaned the tub, and then Hannah took her turn. About an hour after Hannah had taken her bath, my mom called for me. I met her in the bathroom, and she closed the door so no one could hear our conversation. In a quiet voice, she led me to the bathtub and said, "Susie, Hannah didn't clean the tub after she bathed. It's okay because she's our guest, and I'll clean it for her. But I want you to remember what this looks like so that you'll never make the same mistake when you go to other people's homes. Always clean up after yourself. It's just the right thing to do."

Hannah never knew that Mom cleaned the tub, and I'm guessing that Hannah hadn't been taught to clean the tub in her own home. But it made an unforgettable impression on me. I determined to leave someone's house as clean as possible when I was a guest.

Today when I stay in someone's home, I remove the sheets from the bed as I'm leaving and ask if I can put them in the washer. I gather the towels I've used and take them to the washer as well. I empty the trash I've collected in the bathroom wastebasket, as well as from the room I've stayed in, and I try to leave the house with as little work for my hostess as possible.

Why is this important? Because it shows you care. It's an extension of God's love. Do as much as you can for someone. Make it an enjoyable experience so they'll want to have you back. Determine to be the greatest guest possible. Try to go overboard in treating someone else's home and furnishings with great care.

Cleaning up after yourself also shows that you care about the image you portray. By doing so, you're demonstrating the importance of giving and being your very best.

Those who often leave the worst impression as guests are celebrities. Many well-known stars have trashed hotel rooms for years. In 2012 actress Lindsay Lohan caused $50,000 worth of damage to her suite in New York's Union Square W Hotel. She left the floor so covered in cigarette burns that the carpet had to be replaced. I'm guessing she didn't clean the bathtub either. It took the staff months to get the room back to normal.

Back in 1994 actor Johnny Depp was arrested for the damage he caused in his hotel room. Guests heard wood breaking, screaming, and shattered glass. When the police arrived, Johnny was sitting on the floor in the midst of the mess and was charged $9,767 for the damage. [See usmagazine.com (January 15, 2013); cbsnews.com (August 2011).]

Why would someone cause almost $10,000 worth of damage to a place that's not his own? He obviously didn't care about someone else's property. Why would someone burn the carpet in her rented suite? If it doesn't belong to her, it must not matter.

What does this say about character? Integrity? Concern for others?

Clean the bathtub! It'll assist you in developing good clean habits in your own home and also help you become the caring and kind person God wants you to be when you're a guest.

—Susie

FROM GOD:

"In the same way, let your light shine before others, so that they may see your good works and give glory to your Father who is in heaven." (Matthew 5:16 ESV)

GO AHEAD—ANSWER:

→ Describe a time you took the initiative to clean something. How did it make you feel?

→ Describe a time when you knew you should have cleaned something and didn't. How did you feel?

→ How does it make you feel when someone borrows something of yours and returns it to you without properly cleaning it?

24.
Use Manners and Etiquette

I once spoke with a young woman who purposefully refused to show any kind of etiquette.

"People should like me as I am," she said, "without all the polish."

(I'm not sure if she cleaned the bathtub or not, but based on her attitude, I'd guess probably not.)

We often view etiquette as a set of **rules** about how to act during formal dinners. But etiquette is more than that. Using manners shows respect for others. You're not trying to prove that you're better than others; you're telling others that you care about their presence and their comfort. It helps put them at ease.

Here are a few basic etiquette principles that go a long way:

- *Say please and thank you.* It shows that you appreciate people's time and effort.

- *Look people in the eye when you're speaking with them.* It shows that you care.

- *Greet people; introduce yourself, and introduce new people to those around you.* It shows people that you don't want them to feel alone and awkward.

- *Offer guests something to eat or drink when they come to visit you.* It shows that you value their company and appreciate that they took the time to come to see you.

- *Wait until everyone is served before eating. (Unless the host or hostess begins first—then it's okay to start.)* This shows you don't want anyone to feel left out or rushed while eating if the food takes awhile in getting served to everyone.

So, etiquette isn't just about making you look good; it's about focusing on others and ensuring that they feel comfortable and valued.

-Kristin

FROM GOD:

Honor everyone. (1 Peter 2:17 ESV)

GO AHEAD—ANSWER:

→ Have you ever taken any etiquette classes?

→ Have you seen people who don't use manners? How do they come across?

→ How are you doing with your manners and etiquette?

FROM KRISTIN:

If you want to learn more about "official" etiquette for various situations, Emily Post's Etiquette online is an excellent resource.

FROM SUSIE:

Does this mean I'm not supposed to clip my nails at the table?

25.
Grow Something Different

When I was nine years old, our teacher shared with us the joy of watching things grow. She gave us an assignment: plant a bean in a can or a cup, water it, place it near a window, and watch it grow. I got a bean, put it in a plastic container, and placed it on the windowsill of my parents' bathroom.

Guess what! It actually grew. I was amazed. To think that I could take one small bean, plant it in dirt, and watch it produce more beans, just blew my mind.

It still blows my mind.

It's the miracle of God's power laced with His creativity.

Since then I've planted a variety of things. I challenge you to plant something, too. But don't simply plant the ordinary things—beans, carrots, radishes, or tomatoes. Choose something different—something none of your friends would think of.

Of course, it depends on the environment in which you live. California, Florida, Arizona, and a few other states can grow oranges, but because I live in Oklahoma, I can't. Our environment just isn't suited for it. But here are some ideas for things to plant (again, it will depend on where you live) that your friends may not think of:

- popcorn
- almonds
- grapes
- pumpkins
- cotton
- blackberries
- money

(Okay, I'm kidding about that last one. But because I've always heard that "money doesn't grow on trees," I'd like to see if I can grow it in bushes. . .or maybe vines.)

Every fall I buy a few pumpkins to place on my front porch for decoration. This year I decided I'd grow my own. I got all kinds of pumpkin seeds! I got the kind that produce green, yellow, and gray pumpkins. And I got seeds that produce those weird-looking pumpkins that look as though they have zits all over them. I was so excited!

I watered them every day, and I even prayed for them. They spread and grew to a beautiful foot high. And then something happened. I don't know why, but they suddenly just withered and died. I was heartbroken. But I'm not giving up! I'll try again next year.

My favorite flower is the rose. So I got really creative and ordered some amazing colors from an online plant place. I planted purple, orange, pink, yellow, white, and even green roses. You try it! Plant something out of the ordinary.

Why? Because it gives you an opportunity to see God working right in front of your eyes. Think about it: To see something grow and blossom out of dirt from a seed is magical. Mysterious. Miraculous. It's the creativity of God in action. And sometimes we just need to be reminded that He cares about us so much that He took the time to create color, shape, and mystery.

—Susie

• •

FROM GOD:

The LORD will indeed give what is good, and our land will yield its harvest. (Psalm 85:12 NIV)

GO AHEAD—ANSWER:

→ Have you ever planted anything? If so, what have you planted? How did it turn out?

→ If you could plant anything in the world (regardless of needing a specific environment to make it grow), what would you plant? Why?

→ How can you see God's provision in what we plant and sow?

FROM SUSIE:

I'll plant popcorn if Kristin will take care of the butter. Then we can watch a movie and eat buttered popcorn.

FROM KRISTIN:

Uh. . .I don't know how to grow butter. How 'bout I just buy some microwave popcorn?

FROM SUSIE:

Okay. But you have to rent the movie.

26.
Believe in Angels

There used to be a popular TV show called *Touched by an Angel*. I loved it. It featured three angels as humans who would try to help people during the tough times of their lives. You can still catch it on reruns.

Before *Touched by an Angel* was created, there was another popular show, *Highway to Heaven*, featuring Michael Landon (formerly known as Charles Ingalls from *Little House on the Prairie*), who was an angel on a different assignment each episode. His human friend drove him around the nation in an old car to help those in disaster. I always thought it was odd that the angel had to be driven everywhere he went. But I was still fascinated by the show.

Lots of books have been written about angels. And people often say, "She's such an angel," or "I just know my guardian angel was looking out for me."

While angels are definitely real, there's a danger in becoming obsessed with them. We're to keep our focus on God—not on angels. We don't worship angels. We worship God, and God alone! But because the Bible makes it clear that God created angels to assist Him, it's important that we know they're real.

Dr. Billy Graham wrote a wonderful book on angels called *Angels: God's Secret Agents*. Go online and order a copy! It will encourage and comfort you.

It's exciting to know that God has created these special beings to help His children. I've had some close calls when driving and have often wondered if an angel was standing in front of my car, keeping the other vehicle from hitting me.

The Bible is filled with stories of angels intervening in people's lives and helping them. In Acts we can read about an angel visiting Peter in prison.

> Peter was sleeping between two soldiers, bound
> with two chains, and sentries stood guard at the

entrance. Suddenly an angel of the Lord appeared and a light shone in the cell. He struck Peter on the side and woke him up. "Quick, get up!" he said, and the chains fell off Peter's wrists.

Then the angel said to him, "Put on your clothes and sandals." And Peter did so. "Wrap your cloak around you and follow me," the angel told him. Peter followed him out of the prison. (Acts 12:6–9 NIV)

Peter must have been sleeping soundly for the angel to have to strike him on his side! Can't you just hear Peter snoring? Sometimes when we're awakened suddenly, we're kind of in a daze. This must have been the case with Peter, because he didn't simply jump up, get dressed, and run out of prison. The angel had to *tell* him to get dressed. Peter was obviously too groggy to think on his own.

The exciting thing about this (besides the fact that Peter was freed from prison) is that the angel walked him outside the prison gates to safety. He didn't simply unchain Peter. He freed him *and* guided him! We can be sure that when God sends an angel to assist us, the angel will follow through to completion.

We see the same follow-through in Genesis 19:17. When God sent two angels, disguised as men, to warn Lot to leave the area of Sodom and Gomorrah because He was going to destroy those cities, the angels gave Lot and his two daughters specific directions on where to go.

In other words, they didn't simply scream, "Hey! These cities are goin' down!" They made sure Lot knew where safety was. They pointed to a specific place where Lot and his daughters could hide and be protected.

I hope that comforts you! God cares about you so much that He is willing to send supernatural beings from the supernatural realm to help carry out His plan for you.

Do an Internet search for more stories from the Bible about angels. But remember, we don't worship the angels—we worship our God who created the angels.

—Susie

FROM GOD:

Do not forget to show hospitality to strangers, for by so doing some people have shown hospitality to angels without knowing it. (Hebrews 13:2 NIV)

GO AHEAD—ANSWER:

→ Do you have a favorite TV show, movie, or book about angels? What makes it so special to you?

→ Do you believe an angel has ever assisted you?

→ Will you read some scriptures about angels this week?

FROM SUSIE:

Angels are created supernatural beings. They're not bound by our physical laws of nature (gravity, walls, speed, etc.). They can appear in the physical form of a person or even an animal for a specific time to complete a specific task on assignment from God.

FROM KRISTIN:

I had a hamster-

FROM SUSIE:

No. Don't even go there.

27.
Learn Something Musical

I began piano lessons when I was nine, and I started violin when I was twelve. Though I never became proficient at either—and though I hated practicing—I'm grateful for the time I invested in both. Having a musical background just adds a special sparkle to your life.

When everyone is singing in church, you tend to catch on a little faster during a new song. And when there's an opportunity to participate in karaoke, you'll have a better chance of sounding good.

I taught myself to play the guitar when I was in college, and I played it for the eight years I served as a youth pastor. I have to admit, though, I only learned about seven chords, so everything I played had to fit somewhere inside that range!

Kristin plays the accordion and sometimes even incorporates it into her comedy routines. She also gives piano, voice, and accordion lessons. Music has given her opportunities to participate in fun events and meet unique people. She told me about how she once played in an accordion orchestra (an orchestra made up entirely of accordions). The other members came from all over the world and shared stories of their various childhoods and backgrounds.

Consider getting involved in something musical. Could you join the glee club or choir at school? Does your church have a praise team?

Most music stores sell kazoos. Have you ever played one? They're really fun, and anyone can do it! All you have to do is hold it to your mouth and hum inside of it. You'll get kind of a funny fuzzy sound. Grab a few friends and create a kazoo band!

God loves music! The Bible tells us to make a joyful noise unto Him. Don't dare think, *I can't sing like Mandisa, so my noise won't be joyful to God.* He doesn't listen to notes; He listens to the heart. Any music coming from His children that's directed to Him is a joyful sound to His ears.

Building even a small musical foundation into your life will make you a more well-rounded person.

–Susie

• •

FROM GOD:

Come, let us sing for joy to the LORD; let us shout aloud to the Rock of our salvation. (Psalm 95:1 NIV)

GO AHEAD—ANSWER:

→ What's your favorite musical instrument to hear?

→ If you could become immediately proficient with any musical instrument, which one would you choose?

→ Describe someone you know who is really musical. How has music made them a more well-rounded person?

FROM SUSIE:

I don't play the piano anymore.
But I *do* play the radio.

FROM KRISTIN:

I've played the accordion and piano at the same time. If I can figure out how to grow another arm, I'll add my ukulele, too!

28.
Supplement Your Faith with Virtue

The next six chapters will build on each other. We're going to take a good, thorough look at 2 Peter 1:5–7. In these verses we're told to grow and mature in our faith. According to Peter, if we actively practice the character traits mentioned in these verses, we'll be effective and fruitful in our knowledge of Jesus Christ, and we'll be assured of our salvation.

Before we go on, I want you to read the entire first chapter of 2 Peter. Go ahead. I'll wait.

ooooo

Well, it took you long enough! (Kidding. But even if you took five hours, I'm proud of you for doing it!)

In the passage leading up to these verses, Peter tells us we've been given everything we need pertaining to life and godliness—not just a little piece of what we need but everything. Because we know Jesus and what He's done for us, we should do everything we can to adopt these qualities.

"Make every effort to supplement your faith with virtue" (2 Peter 1:5 ESV).

Let's start with the first quality: faith.

Our relationship with Jesus starts with faith. Our faith begins when we confess and repent of our sins and put our trust in Jesus for our salvation. Faith means trusting God's will and living for Him, not for ourselves. That's faith.

The rest of the traits listed don't make us more saved. Once you've placed your faith in Jesus and have a genuine relationship with Him, He will bless you with assurance of His forgiveness. The rest of the characteristics listed are the fruit of someone whose faith is real.

So, how do we build virtue onto our faith?

Virtues are outstanding moral qualities. They're positive aspects of our personality and character. Virtues help us put our faith into action. Patience, persistence, compassion, encouragement, forgiveness, gentleness, thankfulness, self-discipline, honesty—these are godly virtues we should all work toward.

They don't always come naturally to us, but when we ask God for help and realize the Holy Spirit is living inside us and leading us, we can achieve these qualities and make our faith more fruitful and effective.

-Kristin

. . . .

FROM GOD:

Make every effort to supplement your faith with virtue. (2 Peter 1:5 ESV)

GO AHEAD—ANSWER:

→ What is faith?

→ What is a virtue?

→ What godly virtues do you need to work on?

FROM KRISTIN:

If you keep a spiritual journal like Susie suggested earlier, jot down which virtues you'd like to work on. Then keep track of your progress by recording situations where you used these virtues!

29.
Supplement Your Virtue with Knowledge

". . .and virtue with knowledge" (2 Peter 1:5 ESV).

Our knowledge begins with knowing God.

"The fear of the LORD is the beginning of knowledge" (Proverbs 1:7 NIV).

Fearing the Lord isn't the kind of fear we feel while watching a scary movie or hearing a noise late at night when we're home alone. This fear is one of awe and reverence. We're in awe of God and what He's done and continues to do. It's similar to the awe and wonder we feel when we look out over Niagara Falls or the Grand Canyon. We're overwhelmed by the grandeur and the splendor, but at the same time, we have a healthy respect for their power. As we grow in knowledge, our fear of God grows as well, and as our fear of God grows, so does our knowledge.

The best way to grow in knowledge is to study the Bible. Just as you get to know a friend better the more you hang out, you get to know God better when you read His Word. God reveals Himself to us in a unique and special way in the Bible. We see Him interact with His people; we see His heart and what He values through the principles He gives His people.

We can also grow in our knowledge of God by reading books and listening to sermons. Reading devotions, commentaries, and other studies can enrich our study and help us understand difficult passages. These books shouldn't replace reading our Bible directly, but we can learn a lot from those who have devoted their lives to understanding scripture.

We also learn about God through learning in general. When we take a science class, we're not directly learning about God, but we're indirectly learning about Him by studying His creation and uncovering the mysteries of His designs. Through art we see a small glimpse of the creativity He's entrusted to us. Through history we see the way God has orchestrated the past and has woven stories together. Because all creation belongs to God, all study of it in some way reveals Him.

Finally, we gain knowledge about God through community and experience. When we stay in godly community, we hear stories of His faithfulness, we glean wisdom from those who have walked different paths and experienced different trials than us, and we can share our own lessons and testimonies with others.

-Kristin

• •

FROM GOD:

An intelligent heart acquires knowledge, and the ear of the wise seeks knowledge. (Proverbs 18:15 ESV)

GO AHEAD—ANSWER:

→ How are you acquiring knowledge?

→ List some things you've learned about God recently.

→ How can knowledge strengthen your relationship with God?

FROM KRISTIN:

According to Proverbs, knowledge should be sought more than gold. I've never really sought gold, but I've sought a lot of Chipotle, and I'm sure knowledge should be sought more than burritos.

FROM SUSIE:

I'm actually blessed with knowledge. I know exactly where all the Mexican restaurants are in Oklahoma City.

30.
Supplement Your Knowledge with Self-Control

". . .and knowledge with self-control" (2 Peter 1:6 ESV).

Self-control might be the most difficult trait to develop, especially because the world around us says we should be allowed to do whatever feels good.

Think about all those times you should have stayed quiet but instead contributed to hurtful rumors or said something unkind.

Think about when you should have remained calm and respectful but your temper took over and you lashed out.

Think about all the times you were already full but went ahead and ate an entire box of cookies or half a dozen doughnuts.

Think about when you caved and read or watched something you shouldn't have, and recall the thoughts and shame that accompanied putting those images into your head.

Those are all examples of areas where we can strengthen or exercise self-control.

The wise man said, "A man without self-control is like a city broken into and left without walls" (Proverbs 25:28 ESV). Not having self-control leaves you vulnerable, exposed to temptation and sin.

Self-control acts as a wall around our faith, keeping it safe and resistant to attacks. If we have self-control, we can say no when our peers tempt us to do things we know are wrong. We aren't immune to temptation, but self-control is the muscle that strengthens our ability to stay away from potentially harmful situations. It gives us the strength to do what's right when we're faced with a tempting choice.

Self-control doesn't magically blossom overnight. It requires working through many real-life scenarios. So next time you're faced with a temptation, work that self-control muscle!

–Kristin

FROM GOD:

> [Be] hospitable, a lover of good, self-controlled, upright, holy, and disciplined. (Titus 1:8 ESV)

GO AHEAD—ANSWER:

→ How's your self-control? Where does it need work?

→ What are a few benefits of self-control?

→ Was there a time when you were able to exercise self-control? What was the result?

FROM KRISTIN:

Ask God to reveal where you need more self-control. Ask Him to strengthen you when you're faced with temptation.

31.
Supplement Your Self-Control with Steadfastness

". . .and self-control with steadfastness" (2 Peter 1:6 ESV).

Steadfastness means to fix yourself on a direction and to stand firm in your purpose.

As Christians, our purpose is to glorify God by becoming more like Christ. But that's easier said than done, right? Sure, we all *try* to keep God's commandments, but we keep making mistakes.

This is where steadfastness steps up to the plate. It says, "Even though I keep messing up and it feels like sin is winning, I'm going to keep fighting!"

We stand our ground and continue the fight, no matter the obstacles.

Self-control and steadfastness go hand in hand. As you learn self-control, you'll find it easier to stand firm in your convictions.

Remain steadfast in staying away from tempting situations.

Remain steadfast by attending church consistently.

Remain steadfast by praying daily.

Remain steadfast by not saying mean things to or about other people.

–Kristin

• •

FROM GOD:

Therefore, my beloved brothers, be steadfast, immovable, always abounding in the work of the Lord, knowing that in the Lord your labor is not in vain. (1 Corinthians 15:58 ESV)

GO AHEAD—ANSWER:

→ What does it mean to be steadfast?

→ Are you steadfast in any areas of your life?

→ How can you get better at staying focused on growing spiritually?

FROM KRISTIN:

If you're overwhelmed, pick one area where you want to be steadfast and start there. Look at it as a "project." Say, "This week I'm only going to speak kindly about other people," and then follow through!

32.
Supplement Your Steadfastness with Godliness

". . .and steadfastness with godliness" (2 Peter 1:6 ESV).

For followers of Christ, godliness isn't a final destination. It's a way of life. Godliness means you're living in constant relationship with Jesus. To put it another way—it's seeking God daily. It's letting Him speak into your life.

Godliness means devoting your life to God, and it's because of this devotion that you seek to live in a way that honors Him. It's pursuing other characteristics like self-control and knowledge because you know they bring you closer to Him.

Without godliness, life lacks ultimate purpose. Without godliness, all the commands and instructions in the Bible simply become burdensome rules. Without knowing God and drawing closer to Him, we lose sight of why He calls us to live the way we're supposed to live.

So, how can we live a life of godliness?

First, talk to God daily. Set aside time to pray, but continue talking with God throughout your day. We don't have to wait until we're alone in our room at night to pray. We can speak to God anytime, anywhere. Ask for wisdom when you can't make a decision, or pray immediately for patience when someone acts annoying. Later, when you have more time, you can express your thoughts and heart to God in more detail.

Next, read the Bible. (If there's only one thing you take away from this book, it's this—which is why we keep repeating it!) Read it to learn about God, not just to get something to make you feel better.

Finally, understand that God loves you so, so much. He desires a relationship with you because He's your Father! He wants to spend time with you and hear your thoughts, concerns, joys, and frustrations. He's there to comfort and guide you. He delights in you.

Realizing that your great, loving, just, merciful, and mighty God interacts with you personally pushes you toward godliness.

-Kristin

FROM GOD:

For while bodily training is of some value, godliness is of value in every way, as it holds promise for the present life and also for the life to come. (1 Timothy 4:8 ESV)

GO AHEAD—ANSWER:

→ Explain godliness in your own words.

→ What's motivating you to live a righteous, godly life? Is it because you want to have a check-off list of spiritual accomplishments? Or is it because you know it honors God?

→ Take a moment to seek God and to thank Him for being a loving Father.

FROM KRISTIN:

Sometimes we get so focused on the "to-do" list of Christianity that we forget it's first and foremost a relationship with God.

33.
Supplement Your Godliness with Brotherly Affection

". . .and godliness with brotherly affection" (2 Peter 1:7 ESV).

Brotherly affection refers to family-like relationships. In case you're wondering if this applies to girls, in some translations this verse says to supplement your godliness with "mutual affection" (see NIV).

Mutual affection means both people in the relationship actually like and enjoy one another. It doesn't mean you tolerate the other person's existence because you're commanded to do so. You view the other person as a family member.

Think about how you relate to your family—especially your siblings. Even though they're often loud, bossy, and annoying, you'd do anything for your brothers and sisters. You stick up for them, drop everything to help them, and act goofy with them. Your bond is special because you've gone through the ups and downs of life together. Sure, there's bickering sometimes, but (hopefully) you interact warmly, closely, and inclusively with your siblings.

We're to treat our brothers and sisters in Christ similarly. We're not to exclude them because they're weird or different. We acknowledge we're a spiritual family—we share the blood of Jesus Christ.

But you don't know how annoying and strange some of the people at my Sunday school and youth group are!

We can't love people like this on our own. With the power of the Holy Spirit, though, we can love even the most difficult person.

Loving and supporting your brothers and sisters in Christ shows the outside world the power of the Gospel. When we grieve with them, rejoice with them, go out of our way to help them, include them in our family dinners, invite them over for a holiday knowing they'd be alone otherwise, and look out for their physical and emotional well-being, it points to a powerful and loving God who has included us in His family.

–Kristin

FROM GOD:

Love one another with brotherly affection. Outdo one another in showing honor. (Romans 12:10 ESV)

GO AHEAD—ANSWER:

→ How do you act around your siblings? Are you close? If you don't have siblings, how do you act around those you're closest to?

→ What are some ways you can show brotherly affection to those in your church?

→ Has anyone ever shown this kind of love to you? When?

FROM KRISTIN:

I moved to Los Angeles when I was twenty-one. I didn't know anyone, and the first week visiting a new church, a woman approached me, sat down, talked with me, and invited me to have dinner with her family that week. Ten years later, she and her family are still some of my dearest friends.

FROM SUSIE:

When I was twenty-one, I moved to Conway, Arkansas, to be a youth pastor. I'll never forget the World's Largest Balloon Fight we had one Saturday. We filled balloons with everything we could think of: salsa, shaving cream, ketchup, milk, vinegar, and mustard.

FROM KRISTIN:

Susie, that has absolutely nothing to do with the topic I'm writing about: brotherly affection.

FROM SUSIE:

Sure it does. I affectionately plastered my teens with balloons containing cod-liver oil.

34.
Supplement Your Brotherly Affection with Love

"...and brotherly affection with love" (2 Peter 1:7 ESV).

Well, we've reached the final item on our Christian-growth list: love. (This may be a good time to review #19, "Practice Love.")

Why do you think love is at the end of the list?

I think it's because love binds everything together. If faith is the seed, love is the fruit of full-grown, well-cared-for faith.

When we view others as more important than ourselves, we see the value and uniqueness of each person, and it's easier to seek their interests. We may start showing love out of duty—doing things for others because we know that's the right thing to do (building those self-discipline and steadfastness muscles!)—but eventually we'll genuinely care because we know God cares.

Remember: God is the source of your love. It's not your own power that enables you to love people but the love of Jesus overflowing out of your life. Loving people won't be easy if you're not plugged into God's Word and a strong godly community.

So, let's recap the last seven chapters. We're to grow in faith, virtue, knowledge, self-control, steadfastness, godliness, brotherly affection, and love. We won't get it perfect every time—in fact, we'll probably fail more than we succeed. But don't give up. God's grace covers our failures.

Keep praying.

Keep learning.

Keep loving.

-Kristin

• •

FROM GOD:

May the Lord make you increase and abound in love for one another and for all. (1 Thessalonians 3:12 ESV)

GO AHEAD—ANSWER:

→ Out of all the things on the "list" (virtue, knowledge, self-control, steadfastness, godliness, brotherly affection, and love), which do you have the most trouble with?

→ What are a few ways you can practically love those around you?

→ Ask God to help you mature and grow in your faith.

FROM KRISTIN:

Can you memorize 2 Peter 1:5-7?

FROM SUSIE:

I memorized John 11:35.

35.
Make a Greeting Card

I love to get mail. I mean *real* mail—like from inside the mailbox outside my house. I'm talking about the kind of mail that has been delivered by the mail carrier. And I especially love it when I get a greeting card from a friend. It shows me that someone took the time to select a card just for me, pay money for it, and write a personal note on the inside—again, just for me.

But once in a while, I'll get something even better! Sometimes I'll receive a *handmade* greeting card! For example, each year on my birthday, my friend Pam sends me a card she has made especially for me. I look forward to it every year! The fact that she actually takes time out of her busy schedule to sit down and create something for me is invaluable.

Sometimes she cuts pictures out of magazines and glues them onto the construction paper from which she has constructed the card. Sometimes she uses photos that she took of us in past years. She uses different colors of markers, some glitter—anything she can find to make the card really special.

Have you ever made a card?

You can grab stuff you have around the house—like Pam does—or you can visit a local craft store (Hobby Lobby, Michaels, etc.) and purchase all kinds of card-making materials. You can get rubber stamps, adhesive lettering, special envelopes, stickers, thin wooden pieces shaped like everything from baby boots to animals, and much more.

Once you decide whom you want to make a card for, think about their personality. What do they enjoy doing? Hiking, singing, shopping, movies? Are they involved in soccer, basketball, track? You can design the card specifically to match their personality.

Your note inside the card doesn't have to be long. Sometimes simple messages can be the most powerful. Here are a few examples of what you could write:

- "I'm thinking about you today, and I'm thanking God that you're in my life." (Place things on the card that symbolize happiness: smiley faces, beautiful scenery, laughing babies, etc.)

- "Mom, if I could have chosen any woman in the world to be my mom, I would have picked you!" (Use photos of you and your mom for this card and something symbolic of an event the two of you shared together, such as a movie ticket stub or part of a church bulletin, etc.)

- "Your friendship means the world to me." (Use items to make the card symbolize the world [a globe, a map], or use photos of you and your friend. You may want to make the card out of an actual map—and then glue a little piece of white paper on top for your note.)

- "You rock!" (Include really cool photos of rocks and rock formations. Or get a little box and place a smooth, colored rock inside with your card. You can get these from craft stores.)

- "When I count my blessings, you're at the top of the list." (Include a very creative list of things you're grateful for: popcorn, words that rhyme, puppies, etc., but place your friend's name at the top of the list.)

- "Regardless of the weather, you always bring sunshine to my day!" (Find a photo from a magazine—or from your own collection—of a snowstorm, hail, rain, or a tornado, and place it on the card.)

Does your friend need encouragement? Include a special Bible verse in your card. Do they need prayer? Jot a personal prayer inside.

If you've included some add-ons that make your card a little bulky, you may need to take it to the post office before mailing it to see if it requires extra postage. Want to get really creative? Make the envelope, too!

—Susie

FROM GOD:

Is there any such thing as Christians cheering each other up?
(Philippians 2:1 TLB)

GO AHEAD—ANSWER:

→ When was the last time you received something personal in the mailbox? How did it make you feel?

→ When was the last time you actually put a stamp on something and mailed it? What was it? To whom did you send it?

→ Why do you suppose people don't take the time to mail as much today as they did in the past?

FROM SUSIE:

I'm still waiting on Kristin to send me something in the mail.

FROM KRISTIN:

I'm sending you my bills tomorrow.

36.
Try Something That Scares You

After graduating college, I decided to move to Los Angeles. At just twenty-one years of age, I left the comfort of my small hometown and traveled halfway across the country to pursue my dream of taking comedy and writing classes in hopes of one day writing for a television show.

My move excited me, but it was also kind of terrifying. Could I survive in such a huge city? Would I find parking? Would I be safe? Would I be lonely? Would I be able to keep up with the people who had more talent and experience?

You may not be deciding where to move or which job to take yet, but you can still start to examine the motives behind your choices. That'll help to prepare you for some of the bigger decisions you'll face.

We often make decisions based on what feels safe or gives us peace. But here's the thing: sometimes the right choice doesn't always give you complete peace.

Tension comes with knowing that the right path might be long and difficult. The peace comes from knowing we're in God's will and that He's right there with us the whole time.

We want to make our choices with wisdom, not out of fear. There are lots of reasons to avoid a certain choice—things like lack of money, needing to be near family, wanting to stay in a good church. Fear shouldn't be one of them.

If you're hesitant about taking a certain path, ask yourself: "Why am I afraid of trying this?"

Sometimes fears are reasonable and even good, such as fearing the edge of a cliff. Not trying out for the school play because you're scared people might think you're untalented is letting the fear of human opinion control your decision. (By the way, that's a fear that will grip you for your entire life if you don't continuously pull it out by the roots.)

Avoiding a new youth group because you're scared you'll have to sit by yourself is rooted in the fear of rejection and of the unknown.

You may not be able to control feeling afraid, but you can choose how you react to your fear.

Now that I'm older (I'm in my thirties—and yes, that's old), it's interesting to look back and see how God weaved my past struggles, fears, and failures into where I am today. A few things I still don't understand, but through many of the difficulties and fears, I can see a little glimpse into what God was doing. God's still weaving, and He'll weave the threads of your life into a beautiful tapestry until Jesus returns or you go to be with Him in heaven.

-Kristin

- -

FROM GOD:

The fear of man lays a snare, but whoever trusts in the LORD is safe. (Proverbs 29:25 ESV)

GO AHEAD—ANSWER:

→ What are you afraid of? Is it a good fear or a bad fear?

→ Why is fear so powerful?

→ Go ahead and make a list of all the things you'd like to do if fear wasn't an issue—and start conquering them!

FROM KRISTIN:

I'm afraid of moths. (That seems relevant.)

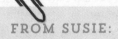

FROM SUSIE:

I'm afraid of washing the dishes. . . so I think I'll just leave them for now.

37.
Develop a Great Handshake

You can tell a lot about people simply by the way they shake your hand. Some handshakes are mousy; they're so flimsy you wonder if the fingers are attached to the hand. And some are so strong they actually hurt. I've had people shake my hand so firmly that my fingers scrunched together and my ring pressed so deeply into the flesh of my finger that I winced. I wanted to say, "Are you trying to convince me you're a superhero? It's not working."

Some handshakes are just icky. These are the kind in which the fingers of the shaker move inside your hand. *Eww.* It feels eerie. Some are sticky—they forgot to wash their hands before shaking. Others are frosty; they feel as though they've just finished building an igloo and rushed inside to shake your hand. Some are not even an actual handshake—the person simply extends a few fingers. That's just weird. There's a reason it's called a handshake and not a fingershake!

And some handshakes just last too long. The shaker either keeps shaking and shaking and shaking your hand. . .or the shaker just holds on to it after the shake is clearly over. I want to say, "Uh, that's my hand. I'd like it back, please. *Now.*"

A good handshake, however, is firm but not so hard your hand goes numb. It lasts only a couple of seconds—enough time to say, "Hi, I'm Susie," or "Great to meet you."

I used to teach speech, drama, English, and creative writing at a public high school. I believe a good handshake is so important that one day I told my speech class they would be graded on their handshake. I went to each student and shook each one's hand. I gave them the perfect handshake and told them their homework was to practice during the weekend. On Monday they returned to class and gave me a great handshake.

Why is a handshake so important? When you're introduced to someone, it can show how interested you are in meeting them. Before or after giving a speech, it can demonstrate how confident you are. And when interviewing for a job, it indicates your confidence.

God wants you to be secure. Of course, your security will come from a deep, growing relationship with Him. But one of the ways you can display that confidence and security is through your handshake.

A great handshake, however, can quickly be destroyed by your facial expressions. Make sure you look in the person's eyes and smile when you shake hands. If you don't, it hints that you're nervous or just not interested.

If you're trying to comfort someone, it helps to give a two-handed shake. After you have their hand in yours, go ahead and place your left hand on top of their hand that's inside your right hand. Elderly people especially like this. It shows great concern. It's like getting hugged through your hands.

I imagine Jesus had the perfect handshake. We know He was often thronged by masses of people. Many of them simply wanted to be touched by Him—to be hugged, to feel His hand on their shoulder, or to place their hands in His.

I imagine Jesus gave a handshake that announced through its firmness, "I am the King of the world," yet was gentle enough to say, "I understand your pain," and warm enough to comfort those in need.

Jesus was confident, strong, and secure. He knew who He was. He wasn't intimidated, never felt insecure, and didn't struggle with self-esteem. And He demonstrated all that every single time He touched someone.

It's time to let others know that you, too, are confident in who you are in our heavenly Father. And you can do that through your handshake.

—Susie

. . . .

FROM GOD:

I want to remind you to stir into flame the strength and boldness that is in you. (2 Timothy 1:6 TLB)

GO AHEAD—ANSWER:

→ When was the last time you shook someone's hand? Who was it? What was the occasion?

→ Have you received a handshake that stands out in your mind?

→ Do you feel uncomfortable shaking hands with someone? If so, practice your handshake until you feel good about it.

FROM SUSIE:

The next time someone shakes your hand, look for the sign around their neck. It's an invisible sign, but you can read it through their handshake. They're feeling obligated to shake your hand, are genuinely interested in you, are insecure, or are confident.

FROM KRISTIN:

I have a special handshake I use with my close friends.

FROM SUSIE:

A fist bump doesn't count as a handshake.

38.
Read Some Classic Literature

Why is it important to read classic lit? Because someday you'll be at a party (it may be ten years from now), and some really smart people will be there. They will have graduated summa cum laude (that means "with highest distinction"—they had superhigh grade-point averages). I graduated *kum ba yah*. Anyway, these really smart people will be discussing stuff that only really smart people discuss. Things like rocket science, computer science, and neuroscience.

And at some point in their conversation, one of them will mention something from a piece of classic literature. For example, Dr. Peabody, who has a degree in molecular science, might refer to the line, "It was the best of times, it was the worst of times" from *A Tale of Two Cities* by Charles Dickens. And if you haven't read that book, his comment will either fly over your head or you'll say something totally inappropriate like, "Yeah, uh, when I went to summer camp, it was totally cool and the best of times because we got to ride horses and eat potato salad and learn archery and spy on the boys' camp across the river. But um, it was also like, uh, the worst of times because I got fifty-seven mosquito bites on my left leg and thirty-six on my right leg, and I broke out all over because of poison ivy, and the showers were icy cold—and it was totally the worst of times."

And Dr. Peabody will think, *Sheesh! Not only does she talk in run-on sentences, but she clearly has not read the classics.*

Or Professor Schlumbach will casually mention character development in *Little Women*, and while he's discussing literary devices such as symbolism, poetic justice, and metaphors, you'll launch into: "Oh yeah! I watch that show all the time. I just love *Little People, Big World*. You know. . .you're supposed to call them little people. It's really cool." And you will have missed the fact that he's talking about a novel written by Louisa May Alcott.

And Dr. Peabody will say something that will hurt your feelings: "It's obvious that you see far more movies and watch way more TV than you read. I'm also guessing that you didn't pay close attention in your literature classes, and you're not very educated."

Ouch. Dr. Peabody's kind of mean. But guess what—that's the impression you'll give if you don't know anything about the classics.

Reading some classic literature will expand your worldview, expose you to some great authors, enable you to carry on an intelligent conversation with smart people, and enhance your general knowledge.

Plus, your teachers will love you!

So here are a few suggestions:

> *Pride and Prejudice* by Jane Austen
> *Black Beauty* by Anna Sewell
> *Silas Marner* by George Eliot
> *Les Misérables* by Victor Hugo
> *1984* by George Orwell
> *The Count of Monte Cristo* by Alexandre Dumas

And here are some spiritual classics:

> *The Pilgrim's Progress* by John Bunyan
> *The Practice of the Presence of God* by Brother Lawrence
> *The Cost of Discipleship* by Dietrich Bonhoeffer
> *Mere Christianity* by C. S. Lewis
> *The Knowledge of the Holy* by A. W. Tozer
> *The Hiding Place* by Corrie ten Boom
> *Christy* by Catherine Marshall
> *Evidence That Demands a Verdict* by Josh McDowell
> *Through Gates of Splendor* by Elisabeth Elliot
> *The Smart Girl's Guide to God, Guys, and the Galaxy* by Susie Shellenberger and Kristin Weber (This is an incredible book that came out a couple of years ago and managed to solve all the world's problems.)

Of course, the most important book to read is the Bible. (For more information, turn to #45, "Read the Entire Bible.")

—Susie

FROM GOD:

Until I come, devote yourself to the public reading of Scripture, to preaching and to teaching. (1 Timothy 4:13 NIV)

GO AHEAD—ANSWER:

→ What's your favorite book of all time? What makes it so special to you?

→ What's the most recent book you've read?

→ What book did you do your last book report on?

FROM SUSIE:

If you get tired of reading, try writing a book—like Kristin and me!

FROM KRISTIN:

I have a sister who doesn't like to read the book because it'll spoil the movie.

39.
Learn to Write

There are a few skills in life that will come in handy no matter where you end up. In the era of shorthand communication, writing is becoming a lost art. Knowing how to put your thoughts clearly, concisely, and creatively onto paper (or into a Word document) will help you not only in school but also in life beyond the classroom.

BRB, LOL, and IDK are fine for texting your friends, but learning to craft *real* sentences using *real* words puts you ahead of the curve.

I once heard a college admissions person say that more than anything else, they're looking for people who can write and communicate.

Even if you don't plan on becoming a writer, it's good to know how to create a good cover letter, send clear e-mails, write reports, or even just have fun wording party invites and Christmas letters.

Here are a few tips for becoming a proficient writer:

1. *Be a reader.* The best writers read all the time. Hopefully after the last chapter we've inspired you to get going on some classic literature, but if you can't get into books, then read magazine articles (not trashy tabloids), newspaper pieces, or anything else that contains names and a story.

2. *Practice, practice, practice.* Journal, write pretend news stories, practice describing things you've seen, write fiction, or pen a play. Join a writers' group in your area or start one. Just keep writing.

3. *Free write.* Writers often get stuck because they keep second-guessing their choices. Free writing simply means you continue to write no matter what. Don't edit or stop to think about what comes next. Pull up a blank Word document or grab a prehistoric pad of paper and pen, and start writing down words without overthinking. Thoughts come now; editing comes later. Here's a small example from some free writing I did awhile back:

Sylvia wanted to see what was over the ledge.

A waterfall? A field? A Chipotle? (Get tomatoes for bean dip.) She couldn't comprehend what she might find, so she simply turned around (Send e-mail to Kathryn about Christmas.) and continued walking. And walking. And walking. (Check on gym memberships.) Until she looked down and realized her feet had turned to raw little nubs because she'd forgotten to put on shoes.

Nothing terribly exciting, but at the very least, free writing reminds me of things I need to get done.

4. *Learn to edit.* Much of writing is rewriting. After free writing, go back through and begin to cut excess wordage. Say what you want to say in as few words as possible. Read your work aloud or ask someone else to proofread it for you. Editing helps you to communicate exactly what you want to communicate to the reader.

–Kristin

• •

FROM GOD:

My heart overflows with a pleasing theme; I address my verses to the king; my tongue is like the pen of a ready scribe. (Psalm 45:1 ESV)

GO AHEAD—ANSWER:

→ Do you ever write? Why or why not?

→ Does writing come easily to you?

→ Why do you think it's a good idea to know how to write?

FROM KRISTIN:

If you get writer's block, just keep. . .

FROM SUSIE:

That's the second time you've used that joke.

FROM KRISTIN:

Great! I can use it one more time before it gets old!

40.
Write a Children's Story

Want a way to put the writing skills you just learned to work? Write a children's story!

Visit your local library and spend a Saturday afternoon reading through some fun children's books. Jot down some ideas from your favorites, and answer these questions:

- Why do children like this specific book so much?

- What has made it stand the test of time?

- What could you create that has some of these qualities but is different from this book?

Then go home and try to write your own children's book! If rhyme is your thing, use it. Let your imagination and your creativity run wild. But first, decide what age group you want to target. That will make a difference. For example, if you're writing for kindergarteners, your story line will be much different than if you're writing for fifth graders.

If you use dialogue, keep it age appropriate. Be careful not to create a plot that's too complicated for a child's mind. Imagine everything in color when you write. Also, strive to hear yourself reading this aloud to a child.

When you've finished your creation, try it out during your next babysitting job. Are the children responsive? Are they engaged in the story? Do they seem bored? Ask your little friends what they liked and didn't like about the story. Encourage them to tell you what would make it even better.

Take your cues from them, and consider reworking your writing. Because children are your intended audience, it's wise to get feedback from as many children as you can.

After you've reworked your story, think about illustrations. If you aren't gifted in artwork, find a friend who loves to draw, and ask them to illustrate your book. Once it's completed, you can take it to Office Depot, Office Max, or another copy place and have it spiral bound.

Or if you're more serious, go online, google self-publishers, and consider getting several copies printed and bound. Then you can sell them or give them to friends and family at special occasions.

Are you familiar with the book *The Outsiders* by S. E. Hinton? Susan Hinton was a high school sophomore when she turned an English class assignment into a young adult novel. It later became a movie starring Tom Cruise.

Hinton went on to write other bestsellers, such as *That Was Then, This Is Now*; *Rumble Fish*; *Tex*; *Taming the Star Runner*; *Some of Tim's Stories*; *Hawkes Harbor*; and two children's books: *The Puppy Sister* and *Big David, Little David*.

Don't ever think you're too young to write a book. Anne Frank began writing her diary when she was thirteen. Even children have written and published books. The key is to become a great reader!

The more you read, the better you'll write. A good reader = a good writer. Grab a glass of lemonade and get your creative juices flowing!

—Susie

• •

FROM GOD:

The plans of the diligent lead to profit. (Proverbs 21:5 NIV)

GO AHEAD—ANSWER:

→ What's your all-time favorite children's book?

→ What makes this book so special?

→ What would you like to teach children through a book of your own?

FROM SUSIE:

When I was in the fifth grade, we were assigned oral book reports. After I read and reported on my assigned book, I then decided to write my own story and give an oral report on it, too. It was called "The Magic Pillow."

FROM KRISTIN:

I once wrote a story about what I thought my hamster did when he escaped from his cage. It was called "The Adventures of Super Rodent."

41.
Contribute to Your Community

How many people do you know in your city or town? How about your neighborhood?

You're not in your community by accident. We're missionaries wherever God has placed us, and your community—which consists of your school, neighborhood, and surrounding areas—is your mission field.

You may live in your community for a short time, or you may spend your whole life in the same ten-mile radius.

Try to live life with this mind-set: Wherever I go I'm going to leave that place a little better than how I found it. Wherever you live, invest your time and talents in a way that helps the people in your community flourish.

It could be helping out with child care during a Bible study or getting a group from your church together to pick up trash at a park or to adopt a highway. It may be helping your neighbor out with their kids so they can run an errand or walking their dogs while they're out of town or at work all day. Maybe there's a Big Brothers Big Sisters program or a food bank in need of volunteers.

Serving in your community gives you a sense of purpose and fulfillment. As we show servants' hearts, we can point people to the one who became a servant on our behalf: Jesus Christ.

-Kristin

• •

FROM GOD:

> Whoever brings blessing will be enriched, and one who waters will himself be watered. (Proverbs 11:25 ESV)

GO AHEAD—ANSWER:

→ Have you ever done a community service project? How did

you feel after it was over?

→ Why should we serve our community?

→ Can you brainstorm and think of a few things you can do to be a blessing to your community?

→ Has anyone in your community ever served you? How did it make you feel?

FROM KRISTIN:

One of my favorite ways to volunteer as a teenager was at community theaters. Not only do you meet a lot of cool people, but you also often get to see the show for free!

42.
Know to Whom You Belong

There are two types of people walking the planet: those who belong to sin and those who belong to God.

People who don't know Jesus belong to sin. Their sin owns them. The Bible says these people are *dead* in their sins. Dead people have no hope—they're not even aware that they're spiritually dead.

The world tries to suck you in and make you believe you should live for something other than God. Satan tries to convince you that God isn't real, that you don't need Him, or that He'd never accept you after what you've done. These are lies Satan uses to keep you chained to sin.

People who know Jesus and put their faith in Him no longer belong to sin. They belong to God. They're part of His family. They're free from the eternal consequences of sin, and they're secure in their spiritual heritage. That means nothing on this side of heaven can truly harm you or separate you from His love.

Before Christ, you were a *slave* to sin.

Fortunately, Jesus came and paid the price for your life. Instead of being a slave to sin, you belong to the family of God. You're His daughter, and you're an heir to His promises.

So if you know and love Jesus, rejoice, because sin no longer owns you!

The best thing about belonging to God is that you don't have to fear the wrath and consequences of your former owner. Your new owner offers you complete freedom in Him.

Freedom from fear.
Freedom from hell.
Freedom from sin.

–Kristin

FROM GOD:

God paid a high price for you, so don't be enslaved by the world. (1 Corinthians 7:23 NLT)

GO AHEAD—ANSWER:

→ Have you ever thought about being a slave to sin?

→ What does it mean to belong to God?

→ Whom do you belong to?

FROM KRISTIN:

When life gets overwhelming, reminding myself that I belong to God brings a lot of comfort.

FROM SUSIE:

When life gets overwhelming, I get a Coca-Cola with crushed ice as I remind myself that I belong to God.

43.
Live Today as Though It's Your Last

None of us knows how long we'll live. But let's pretend that you know how many years you'll be on earth. And let's imagine that you have two weeks left. What would you do in those two weeks?

Would you spend more time with your family? Then go ahead and do that now. What you do isn't as important as simply being together. Baking cookies, filling the car with gas, buying groceries, and going to the cleaners can all be meaningful when they're done with a loved one.

Would you want to make sure they know how much you love God? Then share your faith with them now. Talk about the difference God makes in your life. Share with them the assurance you have that you'll spend forever in heaven with Him because your sins have been forgiven.

Is there anything in your life you need to confess? Make a point to do that today. Is your relationship with Christ where it should be? If not, take time right now to talk with Him. Ask the Lord to reveal anything in your life that's not right. When He brings something to your attention, ask Him to forgive you and give it to Him.

Would you want to be more generous? Right now is a great time to start! Be willing to give your time, your talents, and things you can do (baking cookies for someone, cleaning the house, raking leaves for a neighbor, etc.).

It's interesting, isn't it, that if we knew our lives would end in fourteen days, we'd try to cram all we could into focusing on others and making sure we're right with God? But shouldn't we be doing that *every* day?

Go out of your way today to love others.

Spend more time in prayer.

Perform some random acts of kindness.

We never know how much longer we have. So live today as though it may be your last.

—Susie

FROM GOD:

"You have decided the length of our lives. You know how many months we will live, and we are not given a minute longer." (Job 14:5 NLT)

GO AHEAD—ANSWER:

→ What three people would you want to spend the most time with if you knew your life would end in two weeks? Why these people?

→ What's stopping you from living today as though it were your last?

→ Is your relationship with Christ what it should be?

FROM SUSIE:

If today is my last day, I'm having Mexican food.

FROM KRISTIN:

If it's your last day, I'll *treat* you to Mexican food.

44.
Create a New Drink

Instead of simply drinking a glass of orange juice, why not invent your own individual, favorite drink? Doing this forces you to think outside of the box. I've heard people say, "Susie, I'm just not creative." Guess what—you can *become* creative! In fact, many of the suggestions in this book are actually teaching you how to unleash the creativity that's locked deep inside you.

Play around with ingredients and flavors that you like until you come up with something that tastes great.

This is probably how Cherry Coca-Cola was invented—and Diet Coke with lime. Who knows? Maybe the executives at the Coca-Cola headquarters were sitting around a table having an important lunch meeting when Harold accidentally dropped his lime inside his glass of Diet Coke. And while all the other execs were racking their brains on how the company could increase their profit margins, Harold had a huge smile on his face and said, "Whoa! This Diet Coke with lime is awesome! We ought to market it." And before we knew it, Diet Coke with lime was being sold in grocery stores around the world.

Maybe the next greatest soft drink will be invented by YOU! Here are a few ideas to get you started:

- Have you ever wondered what lemonade and limeade would taste like together? Why not get a couple of frozen cans and find out!

- If tea is your thing, try adding different slices of fruit to it.

- If you have a blender, consider mixing some peaches and blackberries, and then decide which drink you'd like.

- What are your three favorite flavors of ice cream? Put all three into the blender and make a yummy shake.

Consider throwing a "funtastic drink party." Encourage your friends to bring two of their favorite soft drinks, a few pieces of their favorite fruit, and some of their favorite ice cream. Once everything is on the counter, be daring and put your creativity in motion!

Take turns mixing and matching until you each come up with your own favorite new drink. Now give each drink a name (Susie's Splasher, Kristin's Kooler, etc.), and enjoy your refreshing liquid while watching your favorite movie.

—Susie

. . . .

FROM GOD:

This is what I have seen to be good and right: to eat and to drink and be happy in all the work one does under the sun. (Ecclesiastes 5:18 NLV)

GO AHEAD—ANSWER:

→ What's your favorite soft drink?

→ What's your favorite ice cream shake?

→ What's your least favorite thing to drink?

FROM SUSIE:

My favorite soft drink is Coca-Cola. But I also like Dr Pepper with cherry from Sonic with crushed ice. Yum.

FROM KRISTIN:

Sometimes I go wild and put a little ice in my water.

FROM SUSIE:

That doesn't count!

45.
Read the Entire Bible

Beware.

Bold statement coming.

Christians need to read the entire Bible a few times in their lives.

Does that surprise you? If you've never read the Bible from Genesis to Revelation, this statement may make you a bit nervous. But it's important that God's children read what He has said. Think of the Bible as God's personal instruction book to us.

It guides us.

It strengthens us.

It comforts us.

It helps us discern God's will.

Does it bother you when you text, e-mail, or call someone and they never respond? It bothers me. It feels rude. I wonder if God feels the same way when His children don't bother reading the love letter He gave to them.

It's important to read the entire Bible so you'll know what it says. This will help you defend your faith. It will also help you to grow closer to God and to know Him more intimately. Another great reason to read the Bible is to learn our history and to see how God moved through the centuries of time to lavish love, guidance, discipline, and forgiveness on His people.

When I was ten years old, my dad told me something I've never forgotten. He said, "Susie, if you'll just read three chapters every day and read five chapters every Sunday, in one year you'll have read the entire Bible."

You can purchase a one-year Bible with a specific reading plan, or you can simply use the Bible you already have and do it the easy way that my dad taught me. In one of my former churches, our pastor encouraged the congregation to read the Bible through every single year. At the end of the year, the church hosted a giant pizza party for those who completed the challenge.

One year I decided to read the Bible through on my knees. What an experience! Another year I decided to read the whole Bible out loud. It was another great experience. This year I'm reading it while standing on my head—okay, not really. But reading the entire Bible is a blessing—no matter how you do it!

Yes, it will take determination to get through some of the Old Testament books such as Numbers and Leviticus. But before you open the Bible each day, ask God to minister to you even through the detailed, hard-to-understand books. He will!

Go ahead.

Make this your new goal.

Read the entire Bible. And start right now!

—Susie

• •

FROM GOD:

In your hearts revere Christ as Lord. Always be prepared to give an answer to everyone who asks you to give the reason for the hope that you have. But do this with gentleness and respect. (1 Peter 3:15 NIV)

GO AHEAD—ANSWER:

→ What's your favorite Bible verse? Why?

→ Do you have a "life verse" (a verse you or your parents have chosen for your life)? If not, ask God to help you select one.

→ How will reading the entire Bible help you defend your faith?

FROM SUSIE:

I choose different versions of the Bible to read through. The last versions I read were the New International Version and The Message. I'm currently reading The Voice.

46.
Study Even More Apologetics

In our first *Smart Girl's Guide* we gave a few arguments to help you defend your faith.

Often when I speak to teens, they ask me about apologetics. (Apologetics means defending the Christian faith.) They have questions about whether Christianity is true, or someone asked them something they couldn't answer.

Here are a few more common arguments and questions I've heard about Christianity and ways you can answer them:

1. *Christianity is no different than any other religion. All religions are just different rivers leading to the same ocean, right?*

There's one key difference between the God of Christianity and the gods of other religions: all other gods require that you earn their favor by following various laws and rules. Our God extends grace first. It's a free gift. The actions and obedience follow because God changes our hearts—we obey out of gratitude, not obligation. The gift of salvation isn't dependent on our accomplishments. (Thank goodness!) It's also the only religion that gives us confidence of our salvation. Other people cross their fingers and hope what they did was good enough, but they don't know. Because our hope is based on Jesus' work and not our own, we have 100 percent confidence that our salvation is secure.

2. *It's kind of arrogant to say that Christianity applies to everyone, isn't it?*

Christianity deals with the heart, not external behavior, and therefore applies to everyone all over the world. No matter their background, economic status, or education level, everyone's heart is prone to greed, anger, laziness, lying, cheating, and other sins. Because God deals with our hearts, we can seek to be kind, gentle, honest, and selfless, no matter what society we're in. We can worship God with our tribe in Africa or in our room in between homework assignments. We can show kindness by bringing extra water up from a well to help someone in our village, or we can give up Starbucks for a month and donate that money to a homeless shelter. Both show your heart is changed; they're just demonstrated differently.

3. *If evolution isn't true, why do humans and monkeys have so much in common?*

There may be similarities, but when was the last time you threw your poop at someone? (By the way, your answer should be "never" or "when I was one.")

There are physical similarities between humans and monkeys, but couldn't that be evidence of a common creator? There are a few distinct differences between monkeys and humans. For one, monkeys can't discern the difference between good and evil. They can't realize they're sinful and try to become godlier.

Even though we're similar, the things that keep us from being exactly the same as monkeys are huge differences.

-Kristin

• •

FROM GOD:

After this I looked, and there before me was a great multitude that no one could count, from every nation, tribe, people and language, standing before the throne and before the Lamb. (Revelation 7:9 NIV)

GO AHEAD—ANSWER:

→ Do you have questions about Christianity? Have you found answers?

→ Why is it important to know why we believe what we believe?

→ Has anyone ever asked you about your faith? How did you answer them?

FROM KRISTIN:

I love learning apologetics because it gives me confidence and boldness in my faith.

47.
Take Notes in Church

I'm not talking about writing notes to your friends. I'm talking about actually jotting notes down from the pastor's sermon. Many churches have outlines or a fill-in-the-blank page in the weekly worship folder (or bulletin). If your church provides that, go ahead and use it. If not, bring your own notebook.

I've noticed that when I'm taking notes, it forces me to pay attention to what's being said. It makes it harder for my mind to wander if I'm concentrating on writing down what the pastor is saying. It also helps me remember what's being said.

When I take notes, I can refer to them during the week and mentally review the message I heard. This allows the Holy Spirit to continue ministering to me through the scripture that was taught.

If you don't understand something your pastor has said, taking notes gives you the opportunity to research this specific portion later. If you don't write it down, it's easy to forget and never find the answer you needed.

It's fun to keep your church notes together in one notebook and skim through it on New Year's Eve. This will help remind you of what God has taught you throughout the year. Make this a special time of prayer, and thank God for His teaching. Then ask Him to teach you new things during the coming year. He is faithful, and He will do that.

—Susie

• •

FROM GOD:

The whole Bible was given to us by inspiration from God and is useful to teach us what is true and to make us realize what is wrong in our lives; it straightens us out and helps us do what is right. (2 Timothy 3:16 TLB)

→ Have you ever taken notes during church? How has it helped you?

→ What are some other advantages of taking notes on the pastor's message?

→ How can note-taking help you grow closer to Christ?

FROM SUSIE:

I still have some notes from years past (up to a decade ago) that I enjoy reading. And when I do, God ministers to me again.

48.
Back Up Your Computer

Just like humans, technological gadgets don't live forever. It's good to understand how to back up and store your important information and treasured digital memories.

I know just enough about technology not to be Amish. So I'm going to turn this chapter over to my sister, Kathryn, who's an engineer and computer security whiz. (She's built computers and worked with them extensively and knows a lot about this subject.) Dearest readers, I present to you my baby sister!

Hi guys. My name's Kathryn. I'm Kristin's sister. She said she'd buy me Chipotle if I taught you about backing up your computer/phone/iPad/whatever else you use.

Have you experienced losing all your music, pictures, contacts, or homework on your device? It's terrible and creates a lot of extra work for you.

I've had my fair share of electronic mishaps, usually involving water. I've lost a computer to a roof leak and a phone to the depths of the Pacific Ocean. (I really hope a shark picked it up and is enjoying Candy Crush.) Now that technology runs our lives, it's important that we back up important things from our various devices.

First, get an external hard drive. It's like a little safe deposit box for your electronic files. You can usually get them pretty easily on Amazon or at an electronics store. Just plug it into your computer and drag everything you want to save over to it. You might be able to enable automatic backups so it continually backs things up without you having to constantly remember.

You can also get a 'cloud' account, such as Dropbox, Google Docs, or Amazon Prime. Your information is stored in an online server, or a 'cloud.' It may feel like something only grown-ups should worry about, but you're never too young to start keeping track of your important files.

Another simple way to back up your important files is to

e-mail copies of important things to yourself, friends, or family for safekeeping.

If you're working on homework, remember to save your work often. Make it a habit to hit SAVE at the end of every paragraph. This way if Word or PowerPoint crashes (a very common problem on Windows), you know it has been saved, and hours of work won't disappear in the blink of an eye.

It's important to back up your memories and work, but remember that losing your stuff won't be the end of the world. (Unless you had the code to deactivating a world-ending bomb that's set to go off, then by all means, freak out.) You'll see where your heart is and what matters most to you when you almost lose it. In Matthew 6:20 we're reminded that our treasure is in heaven, where moth and rust (or corrupted hard drives and computer viruses) can't destroy it. So be diligent, but remember to back up what truly matters.

-Kristin

• •

FROM GOD:

"But lay up for yourselves treasures in heaven, where neither moth nor rust destroys and where thieves do not break in and steal." (Matthew 6:20 ESV)

GO AHEAD—ANSWER:

→ Do you back up your devices? Why or why not?

→ Have you ever dropped or lost a device? How did you react? If you haven't, how do you think you'd react?

→ What does your reaction to the above question say about where you keep your treasure?

FROM KRISTIN:

My computer kept crashing when I tried to work on this book. Maybe it was a sign. (Or maybe the sign is that I need a new computer.)

49.
Protect Your Identity

While we're on the subject of computers, we're going to chat about a problem that's growing in our society: identity theft.

I'm once again turning things over to my sister, Kathryn, because part of her job involves cyber security and protecting against hackers.

Hey everyone–it's me again. Kristin said she'd buy me as many doughnuts as I could eat if I talked to you about how to protect your identity. (Is it normal for writers to get paid in food?)

Have you ever seen a TV show or movie where someone evil impersonates one of the good guys, doing things that make everyone believe the good guy has turned evil?

These types of stories happen in real life. (Though your experience won't involve helicopter rescues and motorcycle chases. . .hopefully.) It's called identity theft, and it happens a lot.

Thieves steal people's valuable information and use it illegally. They often prey on younger people because they figure most teenagers won't know how to check to see if their information is stolen. (But not you, reader; you'll be prepared!)

Some people create fake accounts using your basic information to get your friends to give them your personal information. (You've probably seen friends on your social media post something inappropriate or bizarre, only to find out they've been hacked.) Others can simply ruin your name and make your life difficult by stealing your credit card numbers, social security number, and other personal information.

Here are a few tips to make sure you're the only you walking around in the world.

Be careful what you post online. Contrary to popular belief, nothing is truly private and nothing actually disappears online, even if you've deleted it. (Even apps like Snapchat, which claims things get permanently deleted, keep a copy of everything sent. Scary, right?)

Trust but verify. Be careful what you tell people over the phone, in chat rooms, or anytime you can't see whom you're talking to. If someone calls, e-mails, texts, or sends smoke signals saying they're supposed to collect certain information, don't send it until you've verified that the person contacting you is indeed supposed to be getting your sensitive data.

Get a special wallet. You may not be old enough for a credit card, but when you get one, you'll probably be given one that has a little chip in it. (Most banks are switching over to this technology.) They're cool, but unfortunately identity thieves can easily steal data off a chip card with a special computer device by getting within a few feet of it. Getting an RFID blocking wallet or credit card sleeve protects against this kind of fraud. You can buy them off Amazon for a few bucks.

Be careful with open networks. An open network, such as the ones in restaurants and coffee shops, allows anyone on that same network to access your information. These networks are convenient but offer no security to protect your username and passwords, credit card information, address, or other personal information. Don't log into your bank, school accounts, or anything else with sensitive personal information. Probably no one is watching you, but it's smarter to wait until you're on a network that's trusted and password protected.

Protect your phone and e-mail address. Where do all your password resets go? Your e-mail. And I'm willing to bet you're always logged into your e-mail on your phone. If someone gets your phone or into your e-mail, they can access all your accounts by doing a simple password reset on any website where you have an account.

Use multiple/different passwords. It's hard to remember things like 8j3Oj@( )294jalkjskjf, but there's an easier way to do it. Choose three random, unrelated words that aren't associated with you. Then string them together as a password: BananaHedgehogDingleberry. Another trick is to take a normal word that you will remember and alter it: bananaphone -> b@NanA9hOne! Don't use any part of your username as your password. Don't use anything as a password that's easy to find on your social media account.

Look out for your friends **and share these tips.**

-Kristin

FROM GOD:

"You keep him in perfect peace whose mind is stayed on you, because he trusts in you. Trust in the LORD forever, for the LORD GOD is an everlasting rock." (Isaiah 26:3–4 ESV)

GO AHEAD—ANSWER:

→ Why is protecting your identity important? Have you thought about protecting it?

→ Are you careful with what you post online?

→ It's important to keep your information safe, but remember your true identity is in Christ, and no one can steal that.

FROM KRISTIN:

If Kathryn asks, please tell her it's normal for writers to get paid in food.

50.
Create Your Own Holiday

Before you were born, one of the most popular sitcoms on TV was a show called *Seinfeld.* You may have seen some of the reruns that are still circulating. In one episode, Jerry's friend George tells his friends about a special holiday his family has.

It was called Festivus. George's dad created it years ago as an alternative to participating in the pressures and commercialism of the Christmas season. Think of it as sort of a fun family rebellion still laced with some celebration. They had a Festivus dinner (meat loaf served on top of lettuce) and a practice called "airing of grievances," in which family members would share disappointing scenarios that had happened throughout the year.

Decorations? Just one: a Festivus pole (an undecorated aluminum pole). This annual event was celebrated by George and his family on December 23.

Even though Festivus is a crazy idea, consider the fun of creating your own holiday! For example, instead of having a normal eighteenth birthday party, why not call it "Susie's Spectacular Shindig" (of course, you'll insert your own name and try to use words that begin with the first letter of your name: Rachel's Radical Reception, etc.).

Instead of accepting gifts, surprise your guests with the flip side. *You* give *them* gifts! Give each person eighteen fun little gifts pertaining to their individual tastes and personalities. Example: Megan loves peppermint ice cream? Purchase a box of ice cream cones from the store and a quart of her favorite ice cream. Wrap eighteen cones and the carton of ice cream for her. Natasha loves Earl Grey tea? Find a special mug and fill it with eighteen bags of Earl Grey. Riley goes bonkers over Butterfinger candy bars? Get eighteen minibars and wrap them in a fun container.

Or create a holiday that has nothing to do with an event that's already on the calendar. Here are some wacky holidays you may not know exist:

- Festival of Sleep Day (January 3)
- Step in a Puddle and Splash Your Friends Day (January 11)
- White T-Shirt Day (February 11)
- Middle Name Pride Day (March 10)
- Reach as High as You Can Day (April 14)
- Lost Sock Memorial Day (May 9)
- Hug Holiday (June 29)
- Take Your Pants for a Walk Day (July 27)
- Wiggle Your Toes Day (August 6)
- Ask a Stupid Question Day (September 28)
- National Candy Corn Day (October 30)
- Stay at Home Because You Are Well Day (November 30)
- Wear Brown Shoes Day (December 4)

Do the above holidays give you some ideas? Anything is possible! Create your own unique, crazy, fun holiday and invite your friends for the party. Make it an annual event!

—Susie

• •

FROM GOD:

A glad heart makes a cheerful face. (Proverbs 15:13 ESV)

GO AHEAD—ANSWER:

→ What's your favorite holiday? Why is this your favorite?

→ What's your least favorite holiday?

→ What's your favorite holiday tradition?

FROM SUSIE:

I love Mexican food, so I think I'll create a Mexican party day.

FROM KRISTIN:

That's already been invented. It's called Cinco de Mayo-May 5.

FROM SUSIE:

Then I'll create a Write a Book Day.

FROM KRISTIN:

That's been created, too. It's called a deadline. And you're late. Hurry up and finish your part of this book!

FROM SUSIE:

Don't worry, I'm on it. (After I make a run to Taco Bell.)

51.
Buy a New Bra

Most females aren't wearing the right size bra for their bodies. How do I know? The bra specialist at Dillard's Department Store told me. Of course, she was trying to sell me a new bra, but she convinced me. And here's another bra fact: You're not supposed to wear the same bra two days in a row. You need two bras so you can alternate wearing each one every other day.

I also discovered that you're supposed to get a new bra every year. It's not a Honda. It won't last for years. Is it time to go bra shopping?

Before the bra was invented, women wore corsets. I imagine they were really uncomfortable, because they extended from below the chest to the hips. Imagine how tough it would be to run, play basketball, or do flips on a trampoline! Maybe corset-wearing women never moved that much. They probably just walked around stiffly and looked miserable.

The corset went out during World War I because lots of women started working outside the home, and wearing a corset was really awkward and impractical. At that time 28,000 tons of metal were being used in the manufacturing of corsets. The US War Industries Board realized that was enough steel to make two battleships!

Bras have gone through several stages of development in past years. Now we have the front-fastening bra, the strapless bra, the sports bra, and bras in a variety of colors. In 2009 a Slovenian company created the Memory Foam Bra. Imagine wearing a miniature Tempur-Pedic mattress on your chest. The bra cups are made of specialized memory foam that moves as you move and reacts to your body temperature.

Having a bra that fits right is really important. You stand straighter and taller. You look and feel better when you're supported correctly. Again, specialists say that chances are good you're *not* wearing a bra that's fitted properly to *you*.

So how can you get the right fit? I suggest going to the lingerie

March 1

Samuel: Hearing God's Voice

1 Samuel 3

mv 1 Samuel 3:19

hwk Read Mark 1:21-39,
    noting a typical day in
    the life of Jesus.

    What was the key for
    him to hear the Father?

department in your favorite clothing store (Macy's, Dillard's, Belk, etc.) and asking a saleswoman if they **employ** a bra specialist. If they do, find out when she'll be working, and make an appointment. This expert will measure your bust, hand you several options to try on, and make sure you receive the proper fit. You'll be surprised with the difference in how you feel and move.

—Susie

• •

FROM GOD:

Women should adorn themselves in respectable apparel. (1 Timothy 2:9 ESV)

GO AHEAD—ANSWER:

→ How many bras do you have?

→ Does your bra still do its job? If not, toss it.

→ Has your body changed during the last year? Time for a new bra.

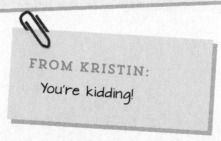

FROM SUSIE:

A few years ago I got an x-ray because I thought I had a broken rib. It hurt to cough, to sneeze, and even to move. The x-ray showed that the wire from my bra was poking through the fabric!

FROM KRISTIN:
You're kidding!

FROM SUSIE:
I'm not kidding! This really happened.

FROM KRISTIN:
I'm not sure I'd admit that.

FROM SUSIE:
We're on deadline for this book, so I'm willing to write about anything!

52.
Keep Up with Current Events

I'm guessing that everyone in North America (and in most of the world—except for those living in a hut somewhere in a village nestled in the bush that hasn't been discovered) know about the devastating events that happened on September 11, 2001—commonly referred to as 9/11.

Imagine what it would be like if you didn't know about this catastrophe? How would it feel to sit in history class while everyone around you discussed it in detail and you didn't have a clue? It's not only important to keep up with what's happening around us—it's also imperative that we're aware of world developments.

Why? Because you need to be "in the know." During our time on earth, we need to know about and understand our surroundings. The more you know, the more aware you'll be of what's happening where you live.

And because it's so easy to keep current, why not be "in the know"? With social media, the newspaper, TV news, and the Internet at our fingertips, we can discover the latest worldwide news in a matter of seconds.

It's easy to become "me oriented" and be content in your own little world. But when I tune in to the news, it reminds me to pray for others around the world who may be facing famine, war, and poverty. Part of being a great conversationalist is knowing what's going on. When you're aware of national and worldwide events, you automatically have something interesting to talk about! Yes, the evening news can improve your social skills.

Did you know that being current on world events can also put you ahead in a job interview? Employers often ask an interviewee for an opinion on a current world event. If you're interviewing for anything in the medical field, it's conceivable that your future employer may ask for your thoughts on Obamacare.

Newscasters and commentators are professionals. This means they use correct grammar, have solid sentence construction, and exhibit polished delivery. Though you're not paying attention to any of that, it's amazing what your subconscious picks up!

Determine to become wise about the world in which you live. You owe it to yourself.

—Susie

. . . .

FROM GOD:

Blessed are those who find wisdom, those who gain understanding. (Proverbs 3:13 NIV)

GO AHEAD—ANSWER:

→ How do you personally benefit from watching the news or reading the newspaper?

→ What's the most current worldwide event that you discussed with someone?

→ How can being current with international happenings impact your confidence?

FROM SUSIE:

Are you familiar with CERN? Get online and discover the fascinating scoop on the Large Hadron Collider. Then start talking about it with your friends. They'll be impressed. I promise.

FROM KRISTIN:

Stay informed, but don't become obsessed or anxious. The news often only puts out negative or catastrophic events. Remember that good things happen a lot, too; but they don't always make the front page.

53.
Go a Day without Makeup

Do you wear makeup? How often?

Every now and then it's good to take a break from makeup and go "au naturel." (Au naturel is a fancy way of saying you're not wearing makeup—you're doing things naturally!)

We're not going to bash makeup or your desire to look nice. However, we need to be aware that we live in a day when we are constantly pressured to look perfect. It's easy to become reliant on beauty products to shape our identity.

Maybe makeup isn't an issue for you, but for many of us our appearance easily becomes an idol. (Remember, an idol is anything that pulls our focus away from God and becomes more important than Him.) We refuse to go into public without putting on our makeup first; we don't want friends to see us until we've applied our mascara; or we quietly judge those who don't put as much effort into their appearance as we do ours.

I consulted my friend Heather, who is a professional makeup artist, and got her thoughts on some practical reasons why we should all take periodic breaks from makeup. Here's what she had to say:

Reason 1. Your face needs to breathe!

The majority of makeup we wear on a daily basis contains toxic, skin clogging ingredients. It really helps your skin and pores when you take a break for a day or two of no gunky makeup.

It's like a workout recovery day (a rest day) for your skin.

If you're having new, major breakouts, it's your skin saying "Heeeeeeelp meeeeee!" Typically, we break out when we've been caking on foundation, contour, powder, and blush. Give your skin a rest day and then use fewer products for a week or so.

Cleanse, apply some moisturizer, and let your face breathe! Finally, drink a lot of water. It's the best thing you can do for your skin.

Reason 2. You'll save time!

Most girls put on anywhere from eight to twenty-five products a day. That's a lot of makeup and a lot of time. Wouldn't it be nice to sleep in a couple of mornings every week?

Reason 3. You'll learn to love yourself on a new level!

Going without makeup even once a week allows you and others to see your natural God-given beauty.

What if they (and you) saw your **darling freckles**, your **amazing** natural lashes, your **uber-cute** dimples, or your perfectly **unique** birthmark?

You might feel exposed at first, like everyone is staring at your "flaws." I promise—no one's even paying attention to them!

It's way more likely that they're focused on your rosy cheeks or supercute smile!

Embrace your unique natural beauty!

-Kristin

• •

FROM GOD:

I praise you, for I am fearfully and wonderfully made. Wonderful are your works; my soul knows it very well. (Psalm 139:14 ESV)

GO AHEAD—ANSWER:

→ Are you an avid makeup wearer? Why or why not?

→ Why do you think it's so easy for girls to become dependent on makeup?

→ Do you think your outer beauty is as important or more important than what's in your heart? (Be honest. You may know the "right" answer to this without believing it or living it out.)

FROM KRISTIN:

We all desire to be beautiful. Ask God to give you contentment with your appearance, and ask Him to help you focus on the beauty that truly counts.

54.
Step Away from the Mirror

While living in Hollywood, I hung out with a family whose kids worked as actors in the entertainment industry. They carved out a nice career for themselves by getting television and movie parts. I knew that other kids and families trying to break into show business envied their success.

As I sat talking with the parents, I watched their son as he passed the hall mirror. He'd stop, fix everything, push his hair back, shake it down, make faces, then lean in and examine his reflection closer. He tried walking away, but it was as if the mirror had a magnetic pull. He kept going back to it.

The boy's parents talked proudly to me of his accomplishments, but I couldn't stop watching their son's interaction with the mirror. He was trapped by his reflection.

It's been many years since this incident, and I've since seen this kid on posters for major movies. On paper he has everything, but I often wonder if his soul feels any sort of fulfillment and satisfaction, or if he's trapped by what he sees in the mirror, on the screen, or in pictures.

Most people aren't much different than this child. We sneak glances in windows and store mirrors and use our photo apps to check our appearance. We take an endless amount of selfies, thinking that capturing the perfect image will somehow give us a little satisfaction and fulfillment.

What's the draw to seeing our own image? What do reflections show us?

Mirrors give us an honest assessment of our outer appearance. We can see and fix flaws. We look into them and feel satisfied and ready to move on, or we hold a grudge against our reflection.

Mirrors also show us the least important, most fleeting part of ourselves. Because society puts a lot of importance on the way we look, it's tempting to try and live up to these standards. The mirror helps us gauge our progress.

We all have physical imperfections. Dwelling on them is pointless unless we're willing to put in the time, money, and effort to fix them. Chances are, however, once you make those changes, you'll find other things that are imperfect and want those changed. It's a vicious cycle.

So use the mirror for what it's meant to accomplish—making sure you're put together and don't have cilantro stuck in your teeth. Try not to let your appearance become your obsession.

It's easy to think our outer appearances are important, but take a moment and think about the people you hang around with. Are you someone's friend *because* of their looks? Probably not. Chances are you like your friends because of common interests and their personalities. Even the most flawless, perfect-looking person can't hide rotten character.

–Kristin

. . . .

FROM GOD:

Let your adorning be the hidden person of the heart with the imperishable beauty of a gentle and quiet spirit, which in God's sight is very precious. (1 Peter 3:4 ESV)

GO AHEAD—ANSWER:

➜ Do you find yourself drawn to your reflection?

➜ How can you avoid becoming obsessed with your looks?

➜ Is it wrong to want to look nice? Why or why not?

FROM KRISTIN:

Don't let the mirror define you. Be defined by Christ alone.

55.
Spend a Few Hours a Week Cleaning and Reorganizing

I don't know about you, but my room can go from perfectly clean to a natural disaster zone in the span of about three minutes. All it takes is for me to second-guess what I want to wear, and within seconds every piece of clothing I own is piled onto my floor as I search for the one shirt I can't seem to find.

You might have had folks tell you to clean up or work as you go. Follow this advice. Staying on top of things makes your world much, much easier, and you'll have fewer stress-related meltdowns. Life is naturally chaotic. When your personal space maintains a little bit of order, it's easier to keep your head above water.

We serve a God of order. The first task God gave to humans was organizing and categorizing His creation. So while we all may function in different levels of organization, we have a responsibility not to live in a state of complete chaos.

We all have those days when we feel like we're treading water. Sometimes I spend the entire day rushing from commitment to commitment, and by the time evening rolls around, things are cluttered and messy. (Or somehow everything I own ends up in my car.)

Set aside a few minutes every morning to put things away and a few minutes in the evening to tidy up.

If you know you're heading into a busy season, try to anticipate what you'll need to do and get those things done ahead.

Realistically you're not going to keep it this way all the time, but if you get in the habit now of cleaning up and organizing as you go, you'll have a much easier time down the road keeping up with what you have to do.

-Kristin

FROM GOD:

> The soul of the sluggard craves and gets nothing, while the soul of the diligent is richly supplied. (Proverbs 13:4 ESV)

GO AHEAD—ANSWER:

→ Are you naturally more organized or disorganized?

→ Why do you think it's important to seek order?

→ How can you stay on top of things?

FROM KRISTIN:

Organizing doesn't come naturally to me. If you're like me, ask a friend who is gifted at organizing to help you establish a system.

FROM SUSIE:

Okay, okay, I can take a hint. I'll help you organize your shell collection.

142

56.
Polish Jewelry and Shine Shoes

This is sort of like making your bed. (We talked about that in our last book. If you haven't read *Smart Girl's Guide to God, Guys, and the Galaxy*, put it on your birthday list!) Making your bed makes you feel "put together" and complete and can even become part of your cleaning and organizing routine. Polishing your jewelry and shining your shoes will do the same (unless your shoes are canvas).

I remember a favorite pair of brown loafers I used to have. They were really classy with a little leather bow. I wore them with slacks and jeans, and because they were my favorite shoes, I wore them a lot.

I had them on at a friend's house and casually remarked that I'd soon need to buy a new pair of loafers because mine were beginning to look shoddy. "Not necessary," she said. "Follow me."

We entered her huge walk-in closet, and I noticed a little stool. "Sit right here," she instructed. Her husband was a pastor, and I couldn't help but notice his Sunday shoes—all shiny and spotless— lined up neatly in a row. She pulled out some shoe polish, wax, and a little rag and began working on my loafers. By the time I left her house, it looked like I was wearing a brand-new pair of shoes!

Some employers take time to notice the shoes of the people they're interviewing. "If he cares enough to keep his shoes looking great, it tells me he'll pay close attention to detail," an executive said.

An employer once told me about a much younger employee. "He's a great speaker. His delivery is solid, people love him, he's very relational, and he's intuitive," the employer said. "But his shoes look terrible."

This may be hard for you to believe, but even though this young employee had several great qualities, his sloppy shoes kept him from advancing in his career. Fortunately, the employer took him aside and taught him the importance of making his feet look good.

Does that sound picky? Think of it this way: Would you take a shower in the morning and wash everything except your feet? No. You wash your whole body. But what's the point in taking time to put on makeup and jewelry and fix your hair if you don't take time for everything? In other words, you wouldn't go to class with jewelry, clean jeans, and a cute shirt but have grime and filth all over your hands.

Nor would you go out to dinner with dirty jewelry. When you take time to polish your jewelry and shine your shoes, you *look* better and you *feel* better about yourself. You feel complete, ready, presentable, and strong. And *that* makes you confident.

Bottom line: Want to feel better about yourself? Shine your shoes and polish your jewelry. Then do it for a friend—just like my friend did for me!

—Susie

. . . .

FROM GOD:

> Therefore do not throw away your confidence, which has a great reward. (Hebrews 10:35 ESV)

GO AHEAD—ANSWER:

→ When you leave the house without making time to look your best, how does it affect your day?

→ When getting ready to go somewhere, what makes you feel complete?

→ Do you know someone who has polished her jewelry? Do you know anyone who has shined his or her shoes? If you've never done this, ask them to teach you.

FROM SUSIE:

When I was five years old, I got tired of my red tricycle and used my dad's brown shoe polish to give it a makeover. I should have left it red. It turned out all blotchy and hideous. It looked kind of diseased.

57.
Iron Something

I was eleven years old when Mom taught me how to iron. I'll always remember her gentle hands wrapped around mine as we gripped the hot iron by the handle. "First iron the collar," she said, as we spread Dad's Sunday shirt across the ironing table. It was fun to watch the wrinkles disappear as the iron slid from left to right.

Most people hate to iron, but I actually enjoy it for three reasons.

1. I get to see immediate results of my work. I don't have to wait a week. I don't have to come back later. It's instant.

2. Because of the mundane routine of the task, I can let my mind wander. This is when my imagination can soar. Creativity unleashes, and I dream about the next book I want to write or a new color I yearn to invent. Routine tasks allow creative people the opportunity to create. I've gone through entire book ideas while ironing.

3. It relaxes me. Ironing is smooth. It's a continuous, uninterrupted exercise.

While it's often a cool thing to wear wrinkled clothes, it's important to know how to iron. You won't always want to look wrinkled. Sure, it's appropriate for hanging with friends, youth group, or school. But at some point you're going to attend something halfway formal. And when you do, you won't want to enter the room covered in wrinkles.

Learning how to use an iron can really come in handy in college. I have a friend who used an iron to make grilled cheese sandwiches in the dorm. You know what else you can do with an iron? When you move furniture, there's always an indentation in the carpet where it used to be. You can run an iron over it, and the indentation will come out!

I love candles. I probably have twenty candles in my house. I love the varying fragrances that fill the rooms. But once in a while, candle wax drips onto a tablecloth or someplace else I don't want it. I use an iron to soften the spilled wax by using a paper bag, towel, and cleaning solution. (Do a quick Internet search to grab the details.)

Do you want to eat a slice of leftover pizza but a microwave isn't available? By placing it on a hot iron and using a blow-dryer on it, you can actually get the same even heat as a microwave.

Are you tired of your carpet stains? By running a hot iron across the stain and using cleaning solution, you can almost always remove the spot.

I travel forty-two weeks or weekends every year as a full-time speaker. Sometimes I travel to tropical places on mission trips. Ironing in this environment is really smart because it kills microscopic fly eggs and larvae that can attach to your clothing if you've hung it out to dry.

The flies lay their eggs on your clothes drying outside, and when you put them on, the eggs hatch because of the heat (from your body as well as the area you're in). The larvae can actually burrow into your skin. *Ewww.* But seriously.

So. . .the next time you're in Cancún, either use the iron in your hotel room, or don't hang your swimsuit out on the balcony to dry.

—Susie

● ●

FROM GOD:

A cheerful heart does good like medicine. (Proverbs 17:22 TLB)

GO AHEAD—ANSWER:

→ When was the last time you ironed something? What was it? Why did you iron it?

→ Can you create a parallel between removing wrinkles from clothing and God removing our sin?

→ How can ironing help you appear professional?

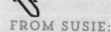

FROM SUSIE:

One time I ironed my pillowcases.
Only. One. Time.

FROM KRISTIN:

I had a friend who ironed her hair because she didn't want to buy a straightener. I haven't been brave enough to try her method.

58.
Know the Ten Commandments

When people are asked if they can name any of the Ten Command-ments, most people rattle off, "You shall not murder." And while that's majorly important, there are nine others that are just as critical.

It's important that we not only *know* these commandments, but that we also make them part of our lifestyle (more on that in #59, "Practice the Ten Commandments"). There's a reason these special ten statements aren't called the Ten Suggestions or the Ten Pieces of Really Good Advice. They are commands directly from God Him-self. And when we abide by them, we're actually more fulfilled and satisfied people.

Can you imagine what it would be like if the entire world lived by the Ten Commandments? Even if humanity only lived with "You shall not murder," it would make an enormous difference! But if the pop-ulace lived by all ten, we would no longer need prisons. Policemen would no longer have to work, and judges would need to find new jobs. If everyone genuinely loved each other, ceased stealing, lusting, coveting, cursing, and demanding their own way, we'd actually live in peace. Our entire world would be flooded with harmony.

You see, God shows us how to love through the Ten Command-ments. He shows us how to live in right relationship with ourselves, others, and Himself.

What are the Ten Commandments? Let's take a quick peek at them as found in Exodus 20:1–17 (esv)!

1. You shall have no other gods before me.
2. You shall not make for yourself a carved image [i.e., idol].
3. You shall not take the name of the LORD your God in vain.
4. Remember the Sabbath day, to keep it holy.
5. Honor your father and your mother.
6. You shall not murder.
7. You shall not commit adultery.

8. You shall not steal.

9. You shall not bear false witness against your neighbor.

10. You shall not covet.

Go through the above list carefully. The Bible tells us that we *all* have sinned (Romans 3:23). So all of us have broken at least one of the Ten Commandments. As you go through the above list, ask God to show you which ones you have broken. Seek His forgiveness, and ask Him to help you build these commandments into your lifestyle.

To be committed to Christ and live by the Ten Commandments is the wisest choice a person can make.

—Susie

• •

FROM GOD:

"If you love me, you will keep my commandments." (John 14:15 ESV)

GO AHEAD—ANSWER:

→ What do you think is the most common commandment broken?

→ How would your life be different if you truly lived by these commandments?

→ Describe someone you know who does live by these commands.

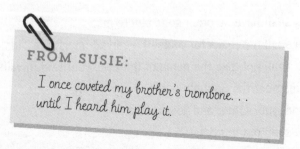

FROM SUSIE:

I once coveted my brother's trombone. . . until I heard him play it.

59.
Practice the Ten Commandments

These special ten commands aren't simply for good reading; they're a great guideline for life. When we adhere to these commands and make them part of our lifestyle, they enable us to live in harmony with others.

Did you know there's often more than one way to look at some of the commandments? For example, it's easy to say, "I haven't murdered. I'd never kill anyone." But you don't have to shoot or stab someone to kill them.

Could you have "killed" someone by ruining their reputation or by gossiping about them? What about killing their hopes or smashing their dreams? Consider for a moment talking with your friends during church. Let's say Jamie really needs to hear what your pastor is saying, but you're texting her, talking to her, or writing notes to her. Could you be committing spiritual murder?

The third commandment tells us not to take God's name in vain. Do you realize that every time you utter, "OMG," you're actually breaking that commandment?

It's easy to claim that we've never stolen anything. And while you'd probably never steal a material item from your friend, have you ever stolen their idea? Could it be that the project you turned in, received an A on, and took credit for was really their brainchild?

Do you truly honor your parents? This doesn't mean you have to agree with them all the time. Do you disagree in a mature and gentle way, or can you be heard screaming and arguing? Because God has placed them in authority over you, it's important that you treat them with respect.

Is there anything in your life that you're spending too much time on, investing too much energy in, or spending too much money on? If so, that could be an idol.

Commit to live a life that pleases God in every way. Ask Him to help you live with integrity—in other words, to practice the Ten Commandments in every area of your life.

—Susie

FROM GOD:

> Nor should there be obscenity, foolish talk or coarse joking, which are out of place, but rather thanksgiving. (Ephesians 5:4 NIV)

GO AHEAD—ANSWER:

→ Is there really a difference between a "white lie" and a lie?

→ Couldn't all forms of deceit be considered lying?

→ Do you live your life in such a way that others see you as trustworthy and honest?

FROM SUSIE:

I wonder if there's such a thing as a purple lie, a burnt-orange lie, or maybe a chartreuse?

FROM KRISTIN:

Is chartreuse even an actual color?

FROM SUSIE:

Yes. It's in the dictionary. It's halfway between yellow and green and was introduced in 1764. Your car is chartreuse.

FROM KRISTIN:

That's a lie.

FROM SUSIE:

Yes, it is—a chartreuse lie.

60.
Treat a Senior Citizen

Many of us in the Western world don't view the elderly as people in other countries see them. In North America we obsess about youth. We use makeup and anti-aging creams, get BOTOX treatments, have face-lifts, and do all we can to appear young.

In Korea the elderly are greatly respected. It's the duty of the younger members of the family to care for their aging family members. This respect extends outside the family unit. Koreans are taught and expected to show honor to the elderly and to view them as authority figures.

In China, too, children are expected to care for their aging parents. In India the elderly are the heads of their families. They often play an important role in bringing up their grandchildren. The younger generation seeks advice from the older family members in just about everything—wedding rituals, financial matters, and interpersonal conflicts. It's the elderly who have the final say.

The aged were viewed as a valuable resource in ancient Rome. Their wisdom and knowledge gained from life experience were appreciated assets to those around them.

Make time to do something special for an elderly person. Is there a senior citizen in your life? Do you have a grandparent nearby whom you can visit? If not, grab a friend and spend an hour at a retirement facility and ask how you can volunteer. Many elderly people would love for you to read to them. Others just want to talk. You don't need to worry about carrying on the conversation—most of the time they'll do all the talking. They simply want and need a listening ear.

Even tiny acts of kindness are greatly appreciated by older folks. Example: My dad is ninety-two and lives in an assisted living facility. It's a great place, and he loves it there. He never has to worry about what to eat or when to wash his clothes—it's all done for him.

I only live twenty minutes from him, so I go over and talk with him, hug and kiss him, read the Bible to him, help him write a letter to his sister, and pray with him.

One thing I always do is clean his eyeglasses. He never thinks about doing it, and if you wear glasses, you know they're easily smudged. I keep a plastic bottle of rubbing alcohol and a cloth in one of his drawers, and I clean them thoroughly. It only takes a minute, but he's always so grateful when he puts them back on.

One evening another older man was sitting at Dad's table in the dining room. His head was bent over his plate, and he was wearing thick glasses. I volunteered to clean them for him. He quickly removed them and gave them to me, and I rushed back to Dad's room and cleaned them with the alcohol and the cloth.

I'll never forget the grin that stretched across his face as he slid on those glasses. "Thank you so much," he said, beaming. "I can see so much better now. This is amazing!"

That simple act of kindness made his day. As I left, I couldn't help but wonder how long it had been since his glasses had been cleaned. It's just something that most people don't think about—cleaning someone else's glasses. And it made him feel as though he were wearing a brand-new pair!

Would you make the time to treat a senior citizen? Your small act of generosity can make a huge positive impact!

—Susie

. . . .

FROM GOD:

"Wisdom is with the aged, and understanding in length of days." (Job 12:12 ESV)

GO AHEAD—ANSWER:

→ Who is the oldest person you know personally?

→ Do you have a grandparent who's still living? If so, when was the last time you communicated with him or her?

→ What's something you can do for a senior citizen this week?

FROM SUSIE:

My ninety-four-year-old aunt announced that she wanted to go to the mall, so I borrowed a wheelchair and drove her to her favorite mall. I wheeled her around the women's department as she selected some new clothes. She had a great time. The next day she decided she no longer liked the clothes and wanted to return them. I took her back to the mall, and we returned every single item. Some days are just like that.

61.
Start Your Own Clique

We're all familiar with cliques.

There might be a clique of mean girls, kids who live on the same street, or girls who have gone to school together since kindergarten.

We look on from the outside and see the "popular kids" hanging out, basking in each other's awesomeness. There's a longing in all of us to be part of the in-crowd. It's the place we believe we'll feel cool, important, and validated.

It's also a facade. (A facade is something that covers up reality. We put facades up when we don't want people to see the "real" us.)

We often spend a lot of time and effort trying to work our way into this inner circle. We long to be noticed and seen by this small, select group of people we, for some strange reason, view as more important than everyone else. We spend mental energy pouting or feeling dejected if we're not included.

I have good news and bad news. Let's get the bad news over with first, and then we'll get to the good news.

Every school, workplace, and club has cliques—even churches have them. They don't go away as you get older. Adults form cliques just as much as kids your age.

The *good* news is that cliques don't have to rule your life.

Yes, it hurts to be excluded. However, you can take that hurt and channel it into positive action and start your own clique.

First, we have to break out of the mind-set that we're missing out on life if we're not included in a certain group of people. There's a huge world with endless opportunities for fun, adventure, and excitement. Why let being excluded by a few people deprive you of that?

Next, there are more people on the outside of cliques than inside them. Make a point to reach out and befriend other people who aren't part of the in-crowd. There are many lonely people out in the world. Probably they're right in front of you, at your school, in your church, and at sports practice, waiting to be heard and seen. If you learn to hear and see the unheard and the unseen, you'll never be without a friend *a day in your life.*

Stop worrying about your social image and start looking for ways to reach out and include people.

Jesus' ministry reached the outsiders. As Christians, our goal shouldn't be to make it into the popular group. Instead, we should seek the heart of Jesus, which is to reach the lost, the ostracized, and the friendless.

Besides, if you're a child of God, you're in the only in-crowd that matters.

-Kristin

. . . .

FROM GOD:

"Learn to do good; seek justice, correct oppression; bring justice to the fatherless, plead the widow's cause." (Isaiah 1:17 ESV)

GO AHEAD—ANSWER:

→ Are there any in-crowds in your school, activities, or church groups?

→ How does it feel to be left out? Why do we feel that way?

→ What are three things you can do to make sure other people feel included?

FROM KRISTIN:

When I was growing up, my imaginary friends and I had a clique. If you were real, you couldn't join. (I was an odd kid.)

62.
Host a Back-to-Childhood Party

Did you know that Kool-Aid is Nebraska's official soft drink? How long has it been since you've had some? Have some fun and travel back in time. Remember when you drank Kool-Aid as a child? Invite your friends to a party in which everything you do reminds you of the fun days from childhood. Serve Kool-Aid in a variety of flavors. What was your favorite food when you were five? Peanut butter and jelly sandwiches? Fish sticks? Corn dogs? Now you have your menu!

If it's possible, create a sandbox or an area in your backyard where you can all play in the dirt. Grab the buckets and scoops, and create as many blocks, castles, walls, and bridges as possible.

Organize some of your most-loved games, such as Red Rover; Mother, May I?; Duck, Duck, Goose; hide-and-seek; or even tag. Then go inside for a cartoon or movie marathon and show your favorites. Any of the Charlie Brown or Disney movies will provide a great start. For an added bonus, serve graham crackers and milk while your friends are engrossed in the movies.

Before the party wraps up, have fun reminiscing by inviting your friends to share the following:

- What's your favorite childhood memory?
- What was your favorite stuffed animal? Do you still have it?
- Were you more afraid of monsters under your bed or monsters in your closet?
- Which did you enjoy more: outside games or indoor ones?
- Who was your best friend when you were young? Are you still in contact with that person today?

—Susie

FROM GOD:

Don't let anyone look down on you because you are young, but set an example for the believers in speech, in conduct, in love, in faith and in purity. (1 Timothy 4:12 NIV)

GO AHEAD—ANSWER:

→ Who was your favorite character to pretend to be?

→ Did you have an imaginary friend? What was his or her name?

→ Which did you enjoy more: splashing in puddles or playing in the dirt?

FROM SUSIE:

We're motivated to view the present and the future in a positive way when we remember and cherish the good times of our childhood.

63.
Do the Dishes When It's Not Your Turn

Have you ever been asked to do something and your immediate response was, "But it's not my turn—I did it last time"?

Or you get in an argument with one of your siblings because you're convinced it's your turn to sit up front, but they are 100 percent certain they haven't sat up front in months.

We're excellent at keeping score, especially when it comes to making sure we're not getting the short end of the stick. We don't want anyone to slack off, and we don't want to shoulder more than those around us.

May I give you a piece of advice?

Instead of spending time and energy making sure everything's 100 percent even, look for ways to set an example for selflessness.

Life isn't fair. There'll be times throughout our lives when the scales won't tip in our favor.

One of my favorite musicals is *Les Misérables*. Perhaps more than any other story I've seen, the story of *Les Misérables* portrays the power of grace. The lead character, Jean Valjean, worked twenty years on a prison chain gang as punishment for stealing bread for his starving family. Valjean, who'd been punished harshly for a minor crime, turned into an angry, bitter man, assuming everyone's purpose in life was to penalize him for his one well-intentioned misdeed.

After serving his time (two decades—basically a lifetime), he gets out of prison and a kind priest offers him food and shelter for the night. That night Valjean steals some of the priest's silver and leaves. The police catch him, and they drag him back to the priest. If Valjean's punishment for stealing bread was twenty years of labor, it's hard to imagine what they'd inflict on him for this crime. Rather than accusing Valjean, the priest tells the police he gave Valjean the silver and proceeds to give him even more.

He not only clears Valjean's name but also gives him the means to start a new life. Valjean treated the priest unfairly. The priest was *owed* his silver. Instead, he allowed himself to lose out on justice to show grace to Valjean and prove to him that there's hope. Valjean was so touched and humbled by the priest's actions that he turned his life around and spent the remainder of his days helping others.

Putting someone ahead of yourself, even when you're owed something, shows there's more to life than getting what's owed to you.

So, do the dishes when it's not your turn, and don't expect anything back. Take the back middle seat joyfully and let someone else sit in the front. Do something to help someone out or to lessen their load, not because it's your obligation or because it's "your turn" but because you care about their soul. This reflects the Gospel. Jesus voluntarily gave up heaven, came to earth, and paid the price for our sins—He did nothing to deserve His crucifixion. His punishment wasn't fair, but Jesus bore this unfairness *for us*. When you voluntarily commit an act of selflessness at the expense of being treated fairly, you demonstrate the character of Jesus.

If life were fair, we'd all get God's judgment, but because life is not fair, we get His mercy.

-Kristin

• •

FROM GOD:

Refrain from anger, and forsake wrath! Fret not yourself; it tends only to evil. (Psalm 37:8 ESV)

GO AHEAD—ANSWER:

→ Have you ever been treated unfairly? How did it make you feel?

→ Have you ever treated someone else unfairly?

→ Why is selflessness so powerful?

FROM KRISTIN:

Our culture views selflessness as weakness. We call selfless people "pushovers" or "doormats." The Bible says the ability to put aside your own agenda to serve others is a gift.

64.
Seek Justice

As mentioned in the preceding chapter, life is not fair.

People get ahead who don't deserve it; others may get more than us without working for it, and sometimes our efforts don't pay off the way we had hoped.

There's a difference between unfairness and injustice. Injustice is unfair, but unfairness isn't necessarily unjust. (Take a moment to process that statement. It's a little confusing.)

Unfairness is your friend getting a fancy car for their birthday when you had to work really hard to buy your clunker. It's unfair, but it's not unjust. Injustice is children sold into slavery. It's unfair *and* it's unjust—in fact, much injustice is rooted in evil.

As Christians, we're supposed to be selfless, but we're also supposed to seek justice and be a voice for the voiceless.

There are two types of reactions to seeing evil in the world: revenge and justice. Revenge means you're angry and you want to get someone back. That's a wrong reaction. Justice means you see people being wronged and you want to help fix the situation. You want righteousness to triumph over evil. Justice includes consequences for those who committed a wrongdoing, but this is different than retaliation. It also includes setting oppressed people free.

Instead of focusing on petty unfairness, focus on how you can help bring justice to those in need. It may be small, like volunteering at a crisis pregnancy center or offering to sell raffle tickets to raise money for an organization that fights human trafficking, but it's work that matters.

-Kristin

He has shown you, O mortal, what is good. And what does the Lord require of you? To act justly and to love mercy and to walk humbly with your God. (Micah 6:8 NIV)

GO AHEAD—ANSWER:

→ What is justice? Why is it important that we seek it?

→ How is injustice different than unfairness?

→ What injustices have you seen in the world? How can you help fix them?

FROM KRISTIN:

Hey, Susie, can you give us some ideas on issues today where girls can help seek justice?

FROM SUSIE:

Absolutely! Just keep reading. . . .

65.
Learn about Human Trafficking

To say this bothers me is a gross understatement. I'm passionate about it. I try to read all I can on it, and I pray for those involved in helping to end human trafficking. It breaks my heart!

Did you know that approximately 27 million men, women, and children are enslaved today? That means there are more slaves now than ever before in history! Although only 6 percent are considered "identified," 800,000 people are trafficked across international borders every year. One million children fall to the commercial sex trade. Of all the world's trafficking victims, 80 percent are women and children. There are currently 161 countries affected by human trafficking, which is a $32 billion per year industry.[1]

What is human trafficking? It's a form of modern slavery that occurs when one person exerts control over another person in order to exploit them economically. In this scenario, the victim is controlled through manipulation, violence, or the threat of violence and can't walk away. Let's break it down into two forms: labor trafficking and sex trafficking.

What's labor trafficking? It includes domestic servants (those who are forced to be household servants), sweat shops workers, and farm laborers who are forced to work without pay.

Sex trafficking is the exploitation of children—as well as teens and adults—who are forced to engage in sex acts for commercialism, fraud, or coercion. Runaway teens are easy targets! Someone who promises to care for their needs but ends up forcing them to have sex, with sometimes several people each day, often lures runaways into prostitution.

Though the two primary areas of trafficking involve labor and sex, people are also trafficked for organ harvesting. And UNICEF estimates that 300,000 children per year younger than age eighteen are currently trafficked to serve in armed conflicts. These are commonly known as child soldiers.

Human trafficking is not just happening overseas. It's in America

---

1. Information in this devotional taken from lawstreetmedia.com.

as well. According to HumanTraffickingSearch.net, the top four states for trafficking are California, New York, Florida, and Texas, but it has been reported in all fifty states.

Talk with your pastor or your youth leader to find out if your church is doing anything to combat trafficking in your city or state. Try to raise awareness at your school. For example, if you're assigned an oral book report, present one about the plight of human trafficking. Or if you're in speech class, ask if you can give your next informative speech on this subject.

Talk about it with your friends and your parents. Consider having some friends over to your house and showing the movie *Taken*. Though it's not a Christian movie, it's definitely an eye-opener about human trafficking and highlights the fact that it can happen to anyone.

Here's a website you may want to check out that has some great information for teens who want to get involved in stopping this atrocity: LetsGetAngry.org.

—Susie

• •

FROM GOD:

Bear one another's burdens, and so fulfill the law of Christ. (Galatians 6:2 ESV)

GO AHEAD—ANSWER:

→ Have you seen any movies about human trafficking? If so, which ones have you seen?

→ As Christians, we have a responsibility to help those who are helpless. Besides those trapped in human trafficking, what others would fall into the category of being helpless?

→ Can you think of a reason not to pray for helpless victims?

FROM SUSIE:

Let's join together in prayer for God to strengthen the ministries and organizations committed to stand against human trafficking.

66.
Do Something about Human Trafficking

What can you do to help? Here are three suggestions:

1. *Become educated.* Learn about human trafficking by reading true stories of people who have survived. These books often give suggestions on how you and your church can help. Here are a few books I recommend: *The White Umbrella* by Mary Frances Bowley; *Enslaved: True Stories of Modern Day Slavery* edited by Jesse Sage and Liora Kasten; *Stolen: The True Story of a Sex Trafficking Survivor* by Katariina Rosenblatt, PhD, with Cecil Murphy; *Passport through Darkness: A True Story of Danger and Second Chances* by Kimberly L. Smith; and *Justice Awakening: How You and Your Church Can Help End Human Trafficking* by Eddie Byun.

2. *Pray.* Prayer is the most powerful weapon Christians have. God actually stopped the sun from moving and gave the earth an extra day when Joshua prayed for more time to win a battle. Through prayer, Hezekiah received an extra fifteen years added to his life! God has raised the dead, rerouted armies, and given barren women children through the avenue of prayer.

3. *Raise awareness.* Consider starting a club in your youth group or at your school. Read some of the books I've suggested and discuss them. While you're together, pray for victims around the world and brainstorm about ways you can raise money to donate to Christian organizations that are working to end trafficking.

4. *Know the organizations.* Do an Internet search and become aware of the Christian ministries involved in fighting human trafficking. Some of the ones I have great respect for are A-21 Campaign, Make Way Partners, and International Justice Mission.

—Susie

FROM GOD:

"Rescue the weak and the needy; deliver them from the hand of the wicked." (Psalm 82:4 ESV)

GO AHEAD—ANSWER:

→ Describe a time when you were unable to help yourself. Who stepped in to give you aid?

→ Identify a time when *you* helped someone who was helpless. How did it make you feel? What was the response of the person you helped?

→ What kind of difference could you make if you looked for ways to help the helpless?

FROM SUSIE:

Here's a book I think you'll love: *One Dress One Year: One Girl's Stand against Human Trafficking* by Bethany Winz with Susanna Foth Aughtmon. When Bethany was in high school, she decided to wear the same black dress every day for one solid year to raise money and awareness about human trafficking. She accessorized the dress in a variety of 366 ways throughout the year (she chose leap year) and raised $8,615, which she donated to six different charities involved in fighting human trafficking.

67.
Learn Good Theology, Part 1

"What comes into our minds when we think about God is the most important thing about us."—A. W. Tozer

When you think about God, what comes to your mind? Do you think of Him as a genie sitting around waiting to give you whatever you want? Do you get a headache trying to wrap your mind around how He's eternal and has no beginning and no end—He's just always *been*? Are you terrified that He's mad at you because of your sin? Do you feel like He's some far off idea, not really caring about you or your life? Do you feel a sense of thankfulness and joy, knowing that He has saved you from your sin?

Out of everything we learn and know, what we understand and believe about God will make the biggest influence on our lives. This is why it's important that we know some *theology*.

Theology means studying the nature of God and understanding our beliefs about Him. Good theology is biblically based. It's not just making up stuff that sounds good. (As we've mentioned before, many people say things about God that sound appealing but actually have nothing to do with what the Bible says about God.) We must test everything against what scripture says about God.

Scripture tells us that God is slow to anger and abounding in mercy. Throughout the Old Testament we see places where God's people sinned and rebelled against Him, and He showed mercy and didn't give them what they deserved.

God is also just. We see God pictured as a judge, and on many occasions we see God punishing those who sin and rebel, because God hates sin. He hates that it separates us from Him, and He hates the sorrow and sadness in the world because of it. Once we understand how terrible sin is to God, we understand why the consequences for it are so severe.

Once we understand why the consequences are so severe, we understand why the price for our sins (God sent Jesus to live a perfect life and die a sinner's death) had such a high price tag.

These concepts sometimes take years of thought and study to understand—and even then we can't fully comprehend them. However, understanding these deep, big-picture theologies gives us a deeper purpose and a better understanding of life.

In the next couple of chapters, we'll go over a few more theological terms and concepts.

-Kristin

• •

FROM GOD:

Have you not known? Have you not heard? The LORD is the everlasting God, the Creator of the ends of the earth. He does not faint or grow weary; his understanding is unsearchable. (Isaiah 40:28 ESV)

GO AHEAD—ANSWER:

→ Do you have questions about God? What are they?

→ What is theology?

→ What comes to your mind when you think about God?

FROM KRISTIN:

The more I learn about God, the more I understand about myself and who I am to Him.

68.
Learn Good Theology, Part 2

Now that you know the importance of theology, let's go over two theologies that lay the foundation for the Christian faith.

The first is called *original sin*. If you've grown up in a Christian household or gone to church, you've probably heard the story of Adam and Eve. (It's found at the very beginning of your Bible in the first few chapters of Genesis.) Adam and Eve were created perfect, and they were placed in a world unstained by sin. When Adam and Eve disobeyed God, they brought a curse into the world. That curse was original sin, and it has been passed down to every single person since. We all are born with a sinful nature. This means that we don't automatically do what's right. We must be *taught* right and wrong, and then be disciplined and guided to consistently do what's right.

Have you ever watched toddlers play? No one has taught them to hit, steal, get angry, and bite when they don't get their way. They naturally react that way. They must be taught to be gentle and kind.

We see the effects of sin all around us. Wars, poverty, and disease are a result of sin in the world.

Once sin entered into the world, we all owed a debt to God to make up for this sin. We needed what's called *atonement*. Sin separated us from God, and we needed someone to repair that relationship, or to atone for it.

We not only needed someone to pay our past debts but our future sin debts as well. Something *had* to be sacrificed to make up for what sin destroyed.

If someone came in and destroyed your house, you could forgive them but you'd still need to pay for the damage already caused. Because God is holy, He needed someone to pay for the damage caused by sin. That's what Jesus did on the cross. He provided payment for sin. He lived a perfect life and kept all God's laws, and then He died the death sinners deserve.

When we accept Christ, we're not only forgiven, but everything is made new in God's eyes. God looks at us and doesn't see sin. He sees the blood of Jesus.

-Kristin

• •

FROM GOD:

> Therefore, just as sin came into the world through one man, and death through sin, and so death spread to all men because all sinned. (Romans 5:12 ESV)

GO AHEAD—ANSWER:

→ Describe in your own words what original sin is.

→ How did Jesus atone for our sins?

→ What questions do you have about original sin and atonement?

FROM KRISTIN:

Think about the areas of your life where you're drawn to sin. Ask God to help you to grow in those areas.

69.
Learn Good Theology, Part 3

Is your brain hurting yet? Great! That means you're thinking! I have two more terms to give you, and then we'll wrap up our trifecta on theology.

We've talked about how sin came into the world and the price paid by Jesus to atone for the brokenness.

But what about the rest of our lives?

It would be nice if the moment we accepted Jesus as our Savior, a switch flipped that prevented us from sinning ever again. Unfortunately, our sinful nature stays with us until we die. We'll always battle anger, laziness, greed, and other sins until we go home to be with Jesus.

However. . .

We now have a weapon living in us that's much, much, *much* more powerful than our sin nature: the Holy Spirit.

The Holy Spirit helps us in our sanctification. *Sanctification* is a fancy word for lordship (which means totally yielding to God's will in every area of your life). As you grow in your faith, you learn how to handle temptation, and you (hopefully) sin less. As you work on your sin and deepen your relationship with God, you'll become holier. Your choices will become more honoring to God. Your words will become kinder. You will focus less and less on yourself.

We become like those we follow; and the longer you follow Jesus, the more you'll become like Him.

This doesn't happen overnight, or even in a year. This happens over the course of our lives. As you read the Bible, pray, and spend time with other Christians, you'll find your heart gradually changing.

A lot of the tips we give in this book are to help and to encourage you on your journey to sanctification.

The war against sin has already been won. Jesus secured our victory when He died on the cross and rose again three days later. Someday there will be a second coming, (that's our second theology term for this chapter, by the way), and Jesus will return and wipe away sin once and for all. Those who trust in Jesus will spend eternity on a new earth—one free from death, sin, disease, lying, cheating, stealing, and everything else that brings hurt and tears.

-Kristin

. . . .

FROM GOD:

Now may the God of peace himself sanctify you completely, and may your whole spirit and soul and body be kept blameless at the coming of our Lord Jesus Christ. (1 Thessalonians 5:23 ESV)

GO AHEAD—ANSWER:

→ Describe *sanctification* in your own words.

→ How has God been sanctifying you lately?

→ What do you think of theology? Do you find it helpful? Why or why not?

FROM KRISTIN:

There are a few starting places to begin learning theology. First, you can get a good study Bible and read the footnotes and explanations. Second, you can get a "first catechism," a book that takes you step-by-step through some basic truths. (Sometimes churches use catechisms, but Google it if you're unfamiliar!) Finally, you can ask your parents, pastor, or youth leader for their recommendations. Your church might have something available for you.

FROM SUSIE:

Understand that sanctification isn't something that will happen automatically. You won't wake up one morning and say, "Hey! I think I got sanctified when I was asleep." It's an actual commitment to lordship.

70.
Visit a Cemetery

This may sound eerie, but it can be a wonderful experience that reminds you of the value of life and the importance of living life to the fullest. Take a friend with you and read what's written on several tombstones. What's the most common descriptive word you see? Is it *mother*? *Father*? *Loved*?

Some tombstones have descriptions on them, such as veteran or minister. What are some of the various descriptions you're seeing? Also, make sure you notice the dates. They usually look something like this: 1950–2015. Obviously, some lived a long life, while others lived only a few years.

But notice the dash between the dates. This small dash indicates the person's whole life. Think about it: An entire life summed up in one dash. Everything they did, all they accomplished, their career, relationships, dreams, money—it's all represented in one small dash.

Life is fleeting. Though we tend to think we have all the time in the world, none of us really knows when our life will end. We *do* know, however, that if we have a genuine relationship with Christ and have accepted His forgiveness for our sins, we will live forever with Him in heaven after we die on earth. This is our hope!

But right now—while we're still alive—God wants us to enjoy an abundant life. So take some time to think about your priorities. What's really important to you? How are you living your life? If you were to die suddenly, what would be written on your tombstone?

Think about *your* dash.

What will be represented in the one small dash on your tombstone? For what do you want to be remembered? What do you want to accomplish?

How can you live an abundant life? By allowing Christ to be in charge. That's right. By yielding to His authority, He gives you peace, fulfillment, purpose, excitement, blessing, forgiveness, grace, and guidance in return.

The most fulfilled people in the world aren't those with all the money and fame, or those who own the biggest house. The happiest people are those who love God, and in turn, they love life. They experience abundance in things that money can't buy. They invest themselves in eternal things.

Check this out: "Store your treasures in heaven, where moths and rust cannot destroy, and thieves do not break in and steal" (Matthew 6:20 NLT).

As you walk through the cemetery, notice the tombstones that mention what was important to the deceased. Some of them will indicate their love for Christ. What will **yours** indicate?

—Susie

• •

FROM GOD:

"I have come that they may have life, and have it to the full." (John 10:10 NIV)

GO AHEAD—ANSWER:

→ What are the three most important things in your life?

→ What changes would you need to make to live a fulfilled life in Christ?

→ How do you want to be remembered?

FROM SUSIE:

Because of the extravagant way God loves me, I want to be remembered as a Christian woman who imitated the One who loved and gave extravagantly.

Chew on this: "The amazing grace of the Master, Jesus Christ, the extravagant love of God, the intimate friendship of the Holy Spirit, be with all of you" (2 Corinthians 13:14 MSG).

71.
Learn How to Discern God's Will, Part 1

When I was seven years old, I wanted to be a nurse. When I realized that would probably involve dealing with blood at some point, my future ambition switched to becoming an explorer. When I realized all the continents had already been explored and claimed, I decided to become a doctor. But I soon discovered I'd have to make good grades in chemistry, science, and biology. (And, also, probably have to deal with blood.) Our career goals often change during our formative years—and even during college.

One of the biggest questions Christians struggle with is knowing God's will. We tend to think of His will in terms of our career—what we'll do for a living. That's only *part* of God's will for our lives. Though God won't unfold His entire plan for your life all at once, you *can* receive clarification from Him about specific direction. Sometimes His direction can take several turns.

By the time I was a senior in high school, I knew I wanted to be a speaker. I yearned to speak to groups of people about God. So following His lead, I got my college degree in speech communications. After graduation, He opened the door for me to become a youth pastor. God began to fulfill my dreams of writing, speaking, and drama within youth ministry. I wrote and directed my own plays, wrote Sunday school lessons, got to disciple teens, and had the privilege of speaking (or teaching) to our group a few times each week.

Later God led me into the public school system. He still fulfilled my desire to speak, because I got to teach five classes with a total of about 130 students each day. I also got to direct plays, and I shared my faith as much as I was allowed to do so.

A few years later, God opened the door for me to create a magazine for teen girls. Focus on the Family hired me to create and be the editor of a monthly publication called *Brio*. After doing that for several years, God led me into full-time speaking and writing. He's still fulfilling the desires of my heart! I absolutely love what I get to do, and I consider it a great privilege.

Check this out: "Take delight in the Lord, and he will give you your heart's desires" (Psalm 37:4 NLT).

It's important to note, however, that I'm not talking about all the material desires we may have: Hey! I'll take a Porsche! And a Jet Ski, a new wardrobe, and a trip to the Bahamas.

God works through our desires to reveal His plan for our lives. In fact, He's the one who placed those desires in our hearts! Take a peek: "May he give you the desire of your heart and make all your plans succeed" (Psalm 20:4 NIV).

God uses the desires He places in our hearts to direct us on the paths He wants us to follow. Chances are good that God isn't going to direct you to do something you hate. He's not going to call me into accounting. He knows I can't even balance my checkbook. He won't ask me to be a math teacher or an astronaut. (Too many numbers.) These aren't the areas in which He's gifted me.

Because He's gifted me in communication skills, He *does* ask me to use those gifts to communicate Him through speaking and writing. He'll also guide you according to the areas He's gifted you. Usually the things you love to do are the areas in which you're gifted.

—Susie

· ·

FROM GOD:

The prayer of a righteous person is powerful and effective. (James 5:16 NIV)

GO AHEAD—ANSWER:

→ Have you prayed about God's will for your life?

→ In what areas has God gifted you?

→ When you dream about your future, what are your greatest desires?

FROM SUSIE:

God always dreams bigger for us than we would ever dare to dream for ourselves.

Let's take a closer look at how we can know God's will. Did you know we can find His will in His Word? This simply means that God speaks to us through the Bible! And God's will for your life will never contradict God's Word.

If someone says, "I just have this impression that I'm supposed to do this. . . ," ask, "Really? Well, what does God's Word say about it?"

"Uh, the Bible says not to do it, but I had this impression from God. . . ."

Hey, if the impression you've had contradicts the Bible, your impression isn't from God! You probably know people who've rationalized being sexually intimate outside of marriage. They're living outside of God's will. In fact, they're sinning, because the Bible tells us to abstain from sex until we're married.

Think for a second about what God's will is *not*:

God's will is not a feeling. There's nothing wrong with feelings. In fact, the Bible says that God has feelings. Feelings are okay, but they're not a sound source for guidance. Feelings can lie! Have you ever made a decision that *felt* like the right thing to do but later proved to be the wrong thing to do?

You can get feelings from being sick, from medication, from fatigue, or from something you ate! You can get feelings from anywhere, so don't base your life on feelings only. Check out what the Bible says: "Who can understand the human heart? There is nothing else so deceitful" (Jeremiah 17:9 GNT). This simply means that our feelings can lie to us; they play tricks on us. The devil can create feelings. Just because you had a feeling doesn't make it valid.

God can work through feelings, but He won't use feelings alone. If He *does* use feelings to communicate with you, He'll also back it up through His Word. This is why it's so important to read the Bible consistently. In fact, if you're not in the habit of reading the Bible daily, please consider doing this. You'll be surprised at the positive difference reading your Bible only **one minute** a day will make!

—Susie

. . . .

FROM GOD:

If any of you lacks wisdom, you should ask God, who gives generously to all without finding fault, and it will be given to you. But when you ask, you must believe and not doubt, because the one who doubts is like a wave of the sea, blown and tossed by the wind. (James 1:5–6 NIV)

GO AHEAD—ANSWER:

→ How often do you read the Bible?

→ Do you have someone in your life who can help you understand the Bible?

→ Will you consider reading and studying the Bible with a spiritually solid adult?

FROM SUSIE:

I'm glad that I began the discipline years ago of reading the Bible each day. It's one of the first things I do when I get up each morning. Before I even have breakfast and leave the house, I first spend some time reading the Bible and talking to God.

73.
Learn How to Discern God's Will, Part 3

Here are some really, really, really, really important things to consider when you're seeking God's will:

1. *It's important to be aligned with the Word and with God's law.* Understand that God isn't going to lead you to go against His will. Swallow this: "I take joy in doing your will, my God, for your instructions are written on my heart" (Psalm 40:8 NLT). Here's where God wants you to search for His will: "Look to God's instructions and teachings! People who contradict his word are completely in the dark" (Isaiah 8:20 NLT).

2. *It's important to spend time in fervent, faithful prayer for guidance.* You can have confidence that if you ask according to God's will, He will hear you! "This is the confidence we have in approaching God: that if we ask anything according to his will, he hears us" (1 John 5:14 NIV).

3. *It's important to keep first things first!* God won't reveal His entire plan for your life all at once. You couldn't handle it all right now. "There is so much more I want to tell you, but you can't bear it now" (John 16:12 NLT). Okay, so you can't know *all* of God's will for your life right now, but you can do what you know is correct right now. Don't stand still. Do what you know is right. You know it's His will that you pray, read the Bible, and grow closer to Him. You know it's His will that you obey Him and learn to love Him more and more. So until He unfolds the entire plan, do this. Then He'll show you what to do next. How do we know He'll show us what to do next? Because the Bible promises He will: "In all your ways acknowledge Him, and He shall direct your paths" (Proverbs 3:6 NKJV).

4. *It's important to discern which of your options will bring the most glory to God.* "Whatever you do, do it all for the

glory of God" (1 Corinthians 10:31 NIV). Spend some time thinking about your options in the above scripture.

—Susie

· ·

FROM GOD:

"For I know the plans I have for you," declares the LORD, "plans to prosper you and not to harm you, plans to give you hope and a future." (Jeremiah 29:11 NIV)

GO AHEAD—ANSWER:

➔ How do you personally hear God's voice?

➔ Have you experienced direction from God through Christian leaders such as your pastor or youth leader?

➔ Describe a time you felt God speaking to you through the Bible.

FROM SUSIE:

I hear God speak to me through music, nature, His Word, Christian speakers, and in my mind and heart.

74.
Learn How to Discern God's Will, Part 4

Let's continue our conversation from the previous pages about some really, really, really, really important things to consider when seeking God's will.

5. *It's important to seek Christian counsel.* The apostle Paul wrote that in the end-times there would be many who had a form of godliness (2 Timothy 3:5, 7–8) and that there would be a lot of false teachers. A good Christian counselor should point you to God's Word—not his or her opinion. "For lack of guidance a nation falls, but victory is won through many advisers" (Proverbs 11:14 NIV). And don't simply seek one person's counsel. I know of a campus chaplain who encouraged a friend of mine to try something that was definitely not biblical. There's safety in a *multitude* of counselors. It would be foolish to place your trust in what even a Christian counselor says if it goes against the Bible. "Blessed is the one who trusts in the LORD, whose confidence is in him" (Jeremiah 17:7 NIV). Seek counsel from Christians, but don't depend on only one person. See if you have several Christian adults saying the same thing—and that it's all supported by God's Word.

6. *It's important that you listen to the voice of the Holy Spirit.* "Whether you turn to the right or to the left, your ears will hear a voice behind you, saying, 'This is the way; walk in it'" (Isaiah 30:21 NIV). That still, small voice that makes you sometimes feel uncomfortable is the Holy Spirit speaking to you.

7. *It's important that you humbly wait on the Lord.* God's timing is different from ours. You can become spiritually stronger by learning the art of waiting on Him. "Be still before the LORD and wait patiently for him" (Psalm 37:7 NIV).

8. *It's important to make and implement a decision.* "Be strong and courageous" (Joshua 1:6 NLT). After you have gone

through all these steps, move forward in the Lord. He *is* with you! As you move forward, watch Him remove the obstacles, and remember that He often requires you to move first. Why? Because this tests and shows you the state of your faith. It requires you to exercise your faith. Joshua had to step into the sea before it became dry land!

9. *It's important that you watch for open or closed doors.* "When I came to the city of Troas to preach the Good News of Christ, the Lord opened a door of opportunity for me" (2 Corinthians 2:12 NLT). Don't worry about what's on the other side of the door. Move forward with your eyes on Jesus, watching for His leading.

10. *It's important to continually seek Him.* You can rest in the fact that God wants you to know His will even more than you do! "But seek ye first the kingdom of God, and his righteousness; and all these things shall be added unto you" (Matthew 6:33 KJV).

—Susie

• •

FROM GOD:

Now to him who is able to do immeasurably more than all we ask or imagine, according to his power that is at work within us, to him be glory in the church and in Christ Jesus throughout all generations, for ever and ever! Amen. (Ephesians 3:20–21 NIV)

GO AHEAD—ANSWER:

➜ Do you feel confident moving forward as you seek God's will?

➜ Has God already revealed part of His will to you?

➜ Will you commit to pray daily for God's will for your life?

FROM SUSIE:

When I was in high school, I made a commitment to God: "Yes, Lord, anytime, anywhere, anything!" Guess what—I've never regretted it! He has taken me to every continent in the world and has given me adventures beyond my wildest dreams.

75.
Make a Decision, Then Stop Stressing

A couple hundred years ago people didn't have nearly as many options as we do today. Travel was difficult, jobs were limited, and choices were few. Many people spent their entire lives within miles of where they were born.

Technological advancements have opened up the world to us. Instead of limited resources, we're now drowning in options. Do I go to college? If so, which one? Where? What do I want to study? Where should I live? Where should I go to church?

Review the four chapters Susie wrote about discerning God's will (#71–74). Pray about it, make a decision using wisdom and the facts you have, and then relax.

We sometimes stress about making the perfect choice—the one that will fulfill and satisfy us perfectly. Even when seeking God, we tend to second-guess ourselves.

Remember: God is always faithful, even when our decision-making skills lack perfection.

Sometimes we assume we've made the wrong decision when times get hard. Things get dramatic in the youth group you chose, the classes at the high school you transferred to are difficult, or the boss at your new job walks all over you.

We're always going to know the problems in the path we've chosen, but we don't know what trials we would have encountered if we'd made a different choice.

God's perfect will for your life is going to happen—not because you're amazing at making decisions but because He loves you and He's faithful.

-Kristin

• •

FROM GOD:

Trust in the LORD with all your heart, and do not lean on your own understanding. In all your ways acknowledge him, and he will make straight your paths. (Proverbs 3:5–6 ESV)

GO AHEAD—ANSWER:

→ Do you have any big decisions coming up?

→ What's a good way to make a decision? What's a bad way?

→ Take a second and ask God to give you wisdom in making choices.

FROM KRISTIN:

I'm terrible at making decisions-except for when it comes to where I want to eat. Then it's Chipotle-always Chipotle.

FROM SUSIE:

I think our friendship is grounded on Mexican food.

FROM KRISTIN:

And sending each other weird things in the mail.

76.
Be Intentional

Very few things in life happen by accident. Musicians don't suddenly know how to play a huge concerto. Athletes aren't couch potatoes one day and Olympic gold medalists the next. Strong, godly Christians didn't just wake up one day really holy. All of those things took deliberate, intentional actions.

Intentionality requires both focus and action. If you want to be more organized, intentionally carve out time each morning to make your bed and tidy up, or spend fifteen minutes each night getting ready for the next day. Focus on what you need to get done and then act on it. Knowing what needs to be accomplished does no good if you don't actually do the work. Intentionally create an organizational system and then stick to it.

If you want to grow in Christ, you must intentionally spend time in the Word, pray, obey, and stay in godly community. When God brings lessons and trials throughout life, intentionally trust that He's using those situations to teach and sanctify you.

If you want to be kind, intentionally seek out opportunities to show kindness. When you're tempted to snap at someone, focus on what you know God has called you to do: respond gently. Intentionally respond with kindness rather than harsh words.

It's easy to look at people who have accomplished great things and envy their skills and merits. Chances are their lives show a pattern of discipline, hard work, and trusting in the Lord.

If you want fast fame, sign up to be on a reality show. If you want to build skills, character, and excellence, then work hard. Dedicate yourself. When you fall down, get back up and keep going. It's difficult sometimes, but well worth the effort.

-Kristin

If anyone, then, knows the good they ought to do and doesn't do it, it is sin for them. (James 4:17 NIV)

GO AHEAD—ANSWER:

→ What are some examples you've seen of people being intentional?

→ How have you been intentional? How could you do better at being intentional?

→ Read James 4:17. What are some situations where you've known the right thing to do and yet not done it?

FROM KRISTIN:

I intentionally finished this chapter and then intentionally ate a cookie. (Actually three.)

77.
Be Flexible

When I lived in Southern California I experienced several major wind-storms. Trees fell and knocked out power, roofs were destroyed, and lawn decorations were relocated to other parts of the city.

However, one tree consistently withstood these storms—the palm tree. Have you seen one? They're very tall and the wood is pliable. During a storm, I'd see palm trees bend almost in half. They looked like they were going to snap, but because they could adapt and bend as the wind gusted, they survived.

Trees that stood tall and strong every other day of the year were often blown over and uprooted in these storms. Why? *They weren't flexible.*

We get pulled in many directions over the course of our lives. (And if we're honest, sometimes even the course of a day can hold many surprises!) We need to be flexible so unexpected situations don't tear us apart.

Sometimes we get our hearts set on something, and when things don't go as planned, we become unhinged. Flexibility requires keeping plans—both small and large—with open palms. We must choose joy, even when we don't get our way.

One winter when I was fourteen, I babysat for a family in my church. I was supposed to be finished in the afternoon, go home, have a few hours of free time, and then go with my family to a Christmas party. I'd meticulously planned my free time. I was going to do some reading, ride bikes with my friends, and then spend plenty of time getting ready to look amazing for the party.

The parents of the kids I babysat were really late getting back, so instead of getting my perfect afternoon, my mom picked me up from the house where I was babysitting with a change of clothes and took me directly to the party.

I'd had my heart set on getting some time to myself and wearing a particular outfit. Instead, I felt rushed and my mom brought a different set of clothes. I was devastated. Instead of acting like a mature, rational person, putting on the green Christmas sweater my mom brought (it was spectacularly tacky—perfect for a Christmas party!) and enjoying good food and friends, I decided to sit in the backseat of our car and cry for most of the party. I made an appearance at the end, but I was so disappointed that plans hadn't gone my way that I'd ruined any chance I had to enjoy the evening. I learned a lot about flexibility that day.

It's hard to face life's disappointments. Sometimes you can't help but feel stressed and overwhelmed by circumstances outside your control. However, you can either roll with the punches (I've heard that phrase many times, but I've never been punched, so I don't have any firsthand insight on that part of the phrase. Rolling, though, is a lot of fun.) or you can grind in your heels and be difficult.

Save your strength from fighting the little things to fight for the important things we're called to stand up for.

–Kristin

. . . .

FROM GOD:

Many are the plans in the mind of a man, but it is the purpose of the Lord that will stand. (Proverbs 19:21 ESV)

GO AHEAD—ANSWER:

→ How can you be more flexible?

→ What are some benefits to being flexible?

→ Now, and perhaps most importantly, can you touch your toes?

FROM KRISTIN:

I can touch my toes. (I know you were wondering.)

FROM SUSIE:

I can touch my nose with my tongue.

78.
Don't Be Afraid to Talk to Guys

Teen girls often tell me they're confused about how to talk to guys. "I'm scared to approach him," "He's just too hard to talk with," and "I never know what to say" are some of their comments.

Ever heard the old saying "Practice makes perfect?" It's true. The more you actually talk to guys, the easier it will be and the better you'll get at doing it. So go ahead and at least say hi to the guys in your halls.

Here are a few conversation tips:

- *Guys love to be complimented.* But they can quickly spot a fake. So you have to actually *mean* it when you compliment a guy. Think about something you can say that's affirming to him. Is he wearing a new shirt that looks good? Tell him. Did he play well in last night's basketball game? Let him know you enjoyed watching. Did you notice him helping someone? Compliment him on that.

- *Guys want to feel confident.* But like anyone, they're afraid of rejection. A guy may not take the initiative to speak to you because he's thinking you'll ignore him or think what he says is stupid. So it's okay to be the first to say hi. That lets him know you're open to a conversation.

- *Guys hate drama.* If you're a drama queen, you probably don't have guys lining up to carry on a conversation with you. They don't want to be involved in personal drama. So if you *have* drama, or if you *cause* drama, make the decision to change.

- *Guys like girls who feel good about themselves.* If you're insecure, or if you're battling low self-esteem, a guy will pick up on that. Learn to feel good about yourself. (God can help you immensely with this because He wants you to live with a great self-image.) When you can laugh at your mistakes—instead of going into panic mode—and stop worrying about your hair so much, guys will perceive you to be confident, and that's a natural magnet. People (yes, that includes guys) will want to be around you.

Establish some good friendships with guys. Don't go gaga and try to make every guy your boyfriend. Just learn to be a great friend! Be trustworthy. Value your friendships. And you'll become more and more at ease in talking with guys.

—Susie

• •

FROM GOD:

A man who has friends must himself be friendly. (Proverbs 18:24 NKJV)

GO AHEAD—ANSWER:

→ Do you have some good guy friends? What's the advantage of having friends who are girls as well as guy friends?

→ What can make it easier for you to start a conversation with a guy?

→ Try looking for something you have in common with a guy you want to talk with. For example, do you share a class together or play on the same coed softball team? Talk with him about commonalities.

FROM SUSIE:

I love having good guy friends because sometimes it helps to get a guy's point of view. (And they can fix stuff for you when it breaks. Thanks, Mark, for fixing my electrical outlet. I had no idea all I had to do was to push the RESET button.)

79.
Put Down Your Phone

How many times do you check your phone over the course of an hour? A day? A week?

Probably hundreds.

If you're like most people in our culture, it's the first thing you look at when you wake up. You can't help but sneak glances at it during class and movies, and you zone out during conversations, wondering how something you posted on Instagram is doing.

Last year I got an iPhone. (I had a flip phone *way* past when it was cool to have a flip phone. My flip phone finally broke, and I became part of the majority and got an iPhone.)

I wasn't immune to the temptation of distraction and constant communication. I found myself compulsively checking text messages, Facebook, and e-mail. A couple of months after getting my iPhone, I was "watching" a movie with my family. Rather than actually pay attention, I put my iPhone in my lap. During the movie I continually snuck glances at it, covertly surfing and responding to texts.

About halfway through the movie, my youngest sister reached over, grabbed my phone, and sat on it.

"Watch the movie," she said.

I was a little embarrassed at having been caught, especially because I speak to teens and tell them not to let their phones rule their lives. I'm glad she had the boldness to call me out on it (even if I wish she hadn't actually sat on my phone), and I've tried to exercise self-control when it comes to my phone.

Why do you think phones are so addicting? It's a chronic problem, not just for girls your age but for everyone.

I have a few ideas why I think they're so powerful. Here are just three:

1. *Phones allow you to control your image.* When you function as a normal human being in society, people witness both your flattering and unflattering moments. They see you smile

and laugh, but they also see you trip, yawn, and spill food on yourself. With selfies and social media, we make sure people see only the best side of us by deleting, precisely posing, and filtering everything we post.

2. *They are a distraction.* Life gets hard. Life gets boring. Life gets annoying. Our phones give us an easy way to escape for a moment. However, these "moments" are getting longer and more frequent and are beginning to take up most of our day.

3. *They provide instant affirmation.* We all long to feel seen, known, and validated. When we post something and the likes, retweets, and comments pour in, we feel important and affirmed. Unfortunately, this affirmation fades quickly and we want to post something else to feel that again. If a post doesn't do well, we feel embarrassed, unseen, and hurt, and we'll remove the post.

These are natural heart tendencies that this abundantly available technology forces us to deal with. Technology isn't bad, but we can use it in good or bad ways. So let's address our hearts and use technology in a way that glorifies God.

And remember:

It's okay to feel bored.

It's okay not to constantly communicate.

It's okay not to have a huge online following.

It's okay if a post doesn't get any response.

It's okay not to know everything right as it happens. (If it's really important, you'll hear about it eventually.)

Now put down your phone and *live*.

–Kristin

• •

FROM GOD:

Those who look to him are radiant; their faces are never covered with shame. (Psalm 34:5 NIV)

→ What are some good uses of technology? What are some bad ones?

→ Are you addicted to your phone? Why?

→ How can you exercise self-discipline with your phone usage?

FROM KRISTIN:

I've seen girls so entrenched in their phones that they miss out on life. Once at a sporting event, a group of girls were so consumed by their phones that they didn't even look up when a great play happened and the rest of the people in the stands cheered. They were so involved with their devices that they missed the excitement of real life happening right in front of them.

80.
Learn to Give a Manicure

Have you ever looked at your nails and thought, *Yikes, what happened there?*

Keeping your fingernails clean and trimmed is part of basic hygiene, and knowing how to give yourself a simple manicure will help keep your digits presentable.

Probably you've already painted your nails or had them painted many times.

If you're able, get a manicure at a nail salon at some point so you can watch and learn from a professional. (Sometimes salons offer manicures for discounted prices on certain days or times, so stay on the lookout for coupons and deals.)

You can buy a basic manicure set from any beauty supply store, drugstore, or grocery store. Pick out your favorite nail polish colors and you're all set. Go crazy! Pick bright, fun colors! Your nails are little canvases for your creative expression.

First, clip your nails to the length you want them.

Then shape them and remove the jagged edges with a nail file.

If you have a cuticle clipper (and steady hands), you can soak your fingers in warm, soapy water for a minute or two and trim your cuticles. If you have shaky hands or aren't precise, ask someone else to do this part for you, because it is incredibly easy to accidentally slip and cut your skin. (I speak from experience.)

Finally—paint your nails! Add a second coat and any extra stickers, art, and pizazz you want.

Why is it good to know how to do a manicure?

1. It's a fun activity to do with your friends when you're hanging out.

2. It's a fun, fairly cheap way to express your personal style.

3. Painted fingernails and toenails are fun to look at. (I've never looked at lime-green nails and felt sad.)

–Kristin

FROM GOD:

So, whether you eat or drink, or whatever you do, do all to the glory of God. (1 Corinthians 10:31 ESV)

GO AHEAD—ANSWER:

→ What's your favorite nail polish color?

→ Have you ever given yourself or your friends a manicure?

→ How can you use manicures and pedicures to bring glory to God?

FROM KRISTIN:

For sanitary reasons, it's a good idea to rinse your manicure tools in warm soapy water every now and again.

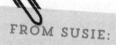

FROM SUSIE:

I tried giving my miniature schnauzers, Obie and Amos, a manicure, but the polish made them sneeze. Plus, they were a little embarrassed.

81.
Learn How to Resist Temptation, Part 1

We're all tempted. No one is exempt. Even Jesus was tempted. He never gave in to temptation, but He totally understands the battle we face when we struggle to say no. He is able to strengthen us and equip us—through His Holy Spirit within us—to say no to temptation. In other words, we don't *have* to give in.

Let's chat about how we can resist temptation. First, when temptation comes your way, run from it! We often think the way to handle temptation is to stand up to it, face it, and not give in. But that's opposite of what the Bible instructs us to do.

Let's listen in on what the apostle Paul told his young friend Timothy: "O Timothy, you are God's man. Run from all these evil things, and work instead at what is right and good" (1 Timothy 6:11 TLB).

Try inserting your name in place of Timothy's, and change "man" to "woman." Then memorize it. This is fantastic ammunition. Paul continued to encourage Timothy to flee from temptation: "Run from anything that gives you the evil thoughts that young men often have, but stay close to anything that makes you want to do right" (2 Timothy 2:22 TLB).

So when you're tempted, remember this excellent advice and run the opposite direction! Did you know that God will always provide a way out of temptation for you? That's great news, isn't it!

Need proof? Here it is:

But remember this—the wrong desires that come into your life aren't anything new and different. Many others have faced exactly the same problems before you. *[Really? I thought I was surely the only one who was tempted with* this. *You mean other people have experienced what I'm struggling with?]* And no temptation is irresistible. *[You're kidding, right? No temptation is irresistible? Wow. I didn't know that. I thought some temptations were so strong that I couldn't help but give in.]* You can trust God to keep the temptation from becoming so strong that you can't stand up against it, for he has promised this and will do what he says. *[Seriously? I feel like belting out the "Hallelujah Chorus" right now!]* He will show you how to escape temptation's power so that you can bear up patiently against it. *[So He really will show me how to escape! Amazing. I never knew this. I think I will sing the "Hallelujah Chorus" right now—a bazillion times. I mean, this is cause for celebration!]* (1 Corinthians 10:13 TLB)

God is faithful.
You can trust Him.
You can depend on Him!
He *will* do what He says.

—Susie

· ·

FROM GOD:

Because he himself suffered when he was tempted, he is able to help those who are being tempted. (Hebrews 2:18 NIV)

GO AHEAD—ANSWER:

→ Is there one specific area in your life in which you're frequently tempted?

→ Is there something that triggers the temptation?

→ How do you most often handle temptation?

FROM SUSIE:

When possible, we may need to remove the source of temptation. Example: A few years ago I found myself watching a TV show that wasn't wholesome. I started watching it from the TV in my bedroom at night when I was trying to go to sleep. God let me know this wasn't His will, so I had the TV removed from my bedroom. I haven't watched the show since.

82.
Learn How to Resist Temptation, Part 2

Let's continue our conversation from the previous pages. With God's help, you *can* resist temptation. You don't *have* to give in. God will always provide a way out. It's important to understand, though, that temptation itself is not sin.

We're all tempted, and even Christ was tempted. But being tempted doesn't mean you're sinning. "For our high priest [that's Jesus]. . .was tempted in every way that we are, but he did not sin" (Hebrews 4:15 NCV).

You see, doing right doesn't lie in the fact that you're never tempted. Don't become discouraged if an evil thought passes through your mind or if an evil desire comes to you. You're not responsible for what flashes through your mind, but you are responsible for how long it lodges there. Someone has said, "You may not be able to stop a bird from landing on your head, but you don't have to let it build a nest!"

Understand that temptation is all about what you allow to keep your attention. Do you want to stay sexually pure until marriage? Then don't spend time alone with your boyfriend in his apartment, his dorm room, or his house when his parents aren't there. Like the old farmer said, "If you don't mean to go into the house, stay off the front porch!"

When temptation comes your way, get away from it. Don't focus on it. Don't allow it to keep your attention. When we give something attention, it results in arousal, and arousal determines action. Here's the proof: "Temptation is the pull of man's own evil thoughts and wishes. These evil thoughts lead to evil actions and afterwards to the death penalty from God" (James 1:14–15 TLB).

Death is the penalty for sin. Thankfully, we serve a God who loves us so much that He will forgive our sins when we repent and ask Him to forgive us. The true meaning of *repent*—in the Greek language in which the New Testament was originally written—means "to completely turn away from." So true repentance isn't, "Sorry, God.

I'll probably do that again tomorrow, but I'll come back and ask You to forgive me again." True repentance is reflected in genuine sorrow for your sins. It's wise to create a plan that will keep you from going down that same pathway again. Establish accountability in your life. Build protective barriers that will keep you away from that specific, sinful pathway, and trust God to provide an escape.

—Susie

• •

FROM GOD:

> Submit yourselves therefore to God. Resist the devil, and he will flee from you. (James 4:7 KJV)

GO AHEAD—ANSWER:

→ What's the danger of playing with a tempting thought?

→ Have you established accountability in your life? If not, will you do so?

→ How can being accountable to a wiser, older spiritual friend help deter you from giving in to temptation?

FROM SUSIE:

I have a handful of friends who can ask me anything at any time in my life. I'm grateful for this valuable accountability.

83.
Trust God

"Just trust God!"

That's a popular phrase often said by Christians to people going through a tough time.

Easy enough, right?

Just trust!

We throw the word *trust* around, but it's often more difficult to put into action. There's no button to press, no switch to flip that turns on our ability to trust God.

So, how do we learn to trust God?

A track record of faithfulness builds trust. Fortunately, God's track record is perfect.

God's track record of faithfulness to you began long before you were even born. It started even before He created the earth. In the Bible, both Peter and John tell us that before the world began, Jesus was appointed to die for our sins (1 Peter 1:20; Revelation 13:8).

Everything you needed to live and inherit eternal life was supplied to you *before the beginning of time*. God's ultimate gift of sacrificing His only Son to grant us entrance into His presence was guaranteed from the beginning.

As you get older and walk with God, you'll begin to see His faithfulness in every situation. You'll begin to see and understand that He works things for our good—sometimes in ways we don't understand immediately. He's building our character, making our faith stronger, and shaping us in a way that glorifies Him.

We're not guaranteed an easy ride on earth. God calls some people to walk very difficult paths, while others He seems to grant fewer trials. One thing, however, is promised to all Christians: no matter your circumstances, God is right there beside you. Nothing, no difficulty or comfort, no good situation or terrible circumstance, no amount of wealth or poverty, can separate you from the love of Christ. That's what our trust in God is built on. And that foundation is unshakable.

-Kristin

FROM GOD:

When I am afraid, I put my trust in you. (Psalm 56:3 ESV)

GO AHEAD—ANSWER:

→ Do you have a hard time trusting God? Why or why not?

→ What is one area where God has asked you to trust Him but you're having a hard time?

→ Ask God to help you trust Him and trust in His will.

FROM KRISTIN:

Trust is sometimes not being able to see the whole path but putting one foot in front of the other anyway, knowing the ground will be there.

84.
Make Everyone Feel Important

A good friend of mine greets anyone who comes to her house with an exuberant hello and a tight, warm hug. Everyone who steps into her home instantly feels cherished and valued.

It's important to make people feel important. It's a gift you can give to anyone—no matter their status.

So, how can you go about treating everyone as important?

First, look them in the eye and give them your full attention. Ask questions about them and their life, and then listen to their responses.

Next, tell people what they mean to you. Don't assume they know you're happy to have them as a friend. Look them in the eye and say, "I'm so glad we're friends," and affirm some of their positive qualities.

Finally, if it's appropriate, give a hug. Touch is a very powerful sense. With just a hand on the shoulder, we can convey loyalty, respect, and appreciation.

A strong, friendly hug from a friend or family member goes a long way. A good hug comforts, encourages, and boosts our senses of connection and community. It communicates safety, acceptance, and care. I've even read about a study saying hugs help ward off the common cold.

So, if you see an elderly woman sitting alone in church, go say hello and give her a hug. It'll mean more to her than you know.

—Kristin

• •

FROM GOD:

Don't be selfish; don't try to impress others. Be humble, thinking of others as better than yourselves. (Philippians 2:3 NLT)

→ Who's made you feel special and important?

→ Have you ever been treated in a way that made you feel like you weren't as important as everyone else?

→ Why should we treat everyone with respect?

FROM KRISTIN:

Tell someone you love that you appreciate them.

85.
Become a Great Conversationalist

I'm sure you've noticed them—the girls who always have a crowd around them. It seems as though everyone wants to be their friend. What's their secret? Why are they so popular?

Here it is: They know how to initiate and maintain a great conversation. That's it. These girls aren't always the best-looking or the smartest. But they've learned the secret of terrific conversation. And being a great conversationalist can open all kinds of wonderful opportunities for you.

Here are a few tips that will help you become a skilled conversationalist.

Don't do all the talking. People like to talk, so give those you're with a chance to do just that! When you hog the conversation, those around you often get bored, annoyed, or eventually just walk away. I have a friend who talks almost nonstop. She's just not comfortable with silence. When we're together, I hardly get a word in. It's no wonder that she doesn't have lots of friends. She just talks too much. Don't make the same mistake.

Learn to ask good questions. A good question is one that demands more than a one-word answer. Saying, "How was your day?" isn't a question that will lead into a conversation because it can be answered with one word: "Fine."

You can still find out about someone's day, but ask the question with a twist: "What was the best part of your day?" This is a surefire conversation starter. You can take your cues from the response and ask more questions—as well as provide input about your own day—that will keep the conversation moving.

Be kind. Refuse to gossip. And don't say negative things about others. Instead, let your conversations be full of grace and kindness. People love to be around someone who makes them feel good about themselves. So kindly compliment the one you're with, and you'll be surprised at how eager they are to keep the conversation going.

—Susie

Let your conversation be always full of grace, seasoned with salt, so that you may know how to answer everyone. (Colossians 4:6 NIV)

GO AHEAD—ANSWER:

→ Take an honest inventory of your conversation with others. Do you tend to do most of the talking?

→ Do people engage easily in conversation with you? If not, look more closely at what you're saying.

→ Are your conversations kind and positive?

FROM SUSIE:

If you try hard enough, you can always find something kind to say to everyone.
"Kristin, that's a very interesting hat."

FROM KRISTIN:

"Thanks, Susie. I think it's made of armadillo."

FROM SUSIE:

"Oh. My."

86.
Give Guys a Break

Guys are just. . .well. . .different. At least they're certainly different from us females. And this is exactly what **attracts** us to them. We're intrigued yet often frustrated with their differences.

While we females tend to **freely** share our emotions, getting a guy to open up about how he feels about something is often like asking him to perform a root canal on himself. **No way.**

And when we say something, guys often interpret it as something completely different.

Girl: Hi, Ryan. How's it goin'?
Guy: Sheesh! Why does she ask me so many personal questions?
Guy: Wanna grab a bite to eat with me?
Girl: Sure! I'd love to go to Greens and Things. I love the variety of salads there.
Guy: Uh, when I say "a bite to eat," I'm usually thinking about Marv's Marvelous Mixture of Meats. Salad isn't in my vocabulary.

Let's give guys a break. Though they're not always on the same page as us, most of the guys in our lives really want to become great men. They desire to be trustworthy and dependable. Guess what—we can help them with that!

When a guy does something **nice** for you, make sure you thank him—even if it's something small, such as holding a door open for you or picking up something you dropped. By verbalizing your appreciation, you build **confidence** in him. You're letting him know that what he did was noticed and that it made a difference for you. This motivates him to continue to reach out in kindness.

God wired men to be the aggressors. Sometimes girls are frustrated because it seems to take some guys **forever** to make the first move. **But be patient.** When a guy wants your attention, he *will* get it. It may not be as soon as you want, but let him make the first move.

Guys may not show as much sensitivity as we do, but give them a break; they're usually quick to respond when we're in need or when they sense danger. Let's learn to appreciate our differences.

—Susie

. . . .

FROM GOD:

> Be completely humble and gentle; be patient, bearing with one another in love. (Ephesians 4:2 NIV)

GO AHEAD—ANSWER:

→ What do you most appreciate about the guys in your life?

→ What's most frustrating about the guys in your life?

→ Do you find yourself making the first move when you like a guy? Consider waiting.

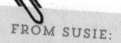

FROM SUSIE:

When we become the aggressor in trying to start a relationship—instead of allowing the guy to do it—we're robbing him of the God-given role our Father created within him.

87.
Study the Book of Revelation

The apostle John wrote the last book of the Bible sometime around AD 95. John was approximately 100 years old. King Domitian hated the Christians—especially John—and unsuccessfully tried to boil him alive. It didn't work, so Domitian banished John to the rocky, volcanic island of Patmos.

It was a gross place filled with criminals and hardly anything to eat. But that's where John received the revelation from God and was told to write this last book of the Bible. (Of course, he didn't know then that it would be the last book.)

If you've never read Revelation, please consider doing so. *But. . .*I encourage you to read the whole Bible first. (See #45, "Read the Entire Bible.") *Why?* Because the book of Revelation has a few more than 500 verses, and 258 of those are directly related to the Old Testament. So that means more than half the book depends on your working knowledge of the rest of the Bible.

Revelation is a fascinating book! It shows us a clear picture of the glorified Christ. And this is completely different from the Christ we see in the Gospels (Matthew, Mark, Luke, and John). The Christ we see there is a willing Lamb being led to slaughter, but in Revelation, He is the *glorified* Christ. He is the Lion of the tribe of Judah. He is in complete control of all that's happening, and He's calling all the shots.

We get comfortable seeing Christ as a cute baby snuggled in a manger and wrapped with warm blankets. But according to 2 Thessalonians, when Christ returns, we'll see Him coming in blazing fire ready to judge those who are against Him.

Revelation deals with the end-times and with what will happen during the seven years of tribulation on earth. It's important that we know this, because it brings an urgency to live for God *now*. There are varying opinions on whether Christians will be removed from the earth before the tribulation or during the tribulation, or whether they will go through the tribulation. Guess what—that's not the issue. The real issue is if your heart is right with God.

Reading the book of Revelation will encourage you to share your faith, because you won't want any of your loved ones to experience the tribulation without God. If we *are* removed before the tribulation, great! If we're not, God is faithful! He has promised never to leave us. So we can depend on His strength to sustain us.

—Susie

. . . .

FROM GOD:

"It is the LORD who goes before you. He will be with you; he will not leave you or forsake you. Do not fear or be dismayed." (Deuteronomy 31:8 ESV)

GO AHEAD—ANSWER:

→ Have you read any books that deal with the end-times or prophecy (e.g., the Left Behind series, *The Harbinger*, *Agents of the Apocalypse*, *The Prophecy Answer Book*)?

→ What comes to mind when you think of the end-times?

→ Will you commit to reading at least one book dealing with this subject?

FROM SUSIE:

It's a fact: Jesus Christ will return. Though no one knows the exact date or time, the Bible gives us specific signs that will point to the general season of His second coming.

88.
Avoid Useless Arguments

Here's the thing: not every battle is yours to fight.

For example, I've had peers "pick" fights by saying things they know I disagree with. Or they'd insult me for believing something while never actually addressing the issues. In fact, often people don't want a discussion; they want to get a reaction out of you.

It's wise to discern whether someone is legitimately searching for answers or simply looking for a fight. Asking good questions will help you avoid useless arguments. A good question tests whether people want to hear your perspective and learn or just argue. When they respond, actually listen to their answers. Don't cut them off or put them down. Pray silently for God to help you understand where they're coming from, and ask Him to give you the best way to respond. (Always respond kindly and gently—even when disagreeing.)

Here are a few examples of questions you can ask to help people clarify their beliefs:

→ "You said you believe all religions serve the same God. If you don't mind me asking, why do you think that?"

→ "You think abortion should be legal. Just out of curiosity, when do you think a baby becomes a person? Why do we call an unborn child a 'baby' when the parents want it, but call it a 'fetus' when it's unplanned and inconvenient? Is someone's value based on whether or not they're wanted?"

→ "You don't think there's anything after life here on earth. What do you think the purpose of life is then?"

This puts the burden on *them* to explain why they believe what they believe. They'll likely be excited to talk about what they've found or discovered. Or, if they're not in the mood to truly talk about the issue at hand, they'll brush it off and you can move on and talk about something else.

Staying calm shows you're confident enough in your beliefs not to get riled up. Christianity can hold its own under scrutiny. (See

#46, "Study Even More Apologetics.")

Ask the Holy Spirit to guide you and to make it clear when to speak up and when to stay silent. Pray for boldness and trust.

-Kristin

• •

FROM GOD:

Have nothing to do with foolish, ignorant controversies; you know that they breed quarrels. (2 Timothy 2:23 ESV)

GO AHEAD—ANSWER:

→ Have you ever been in a foolish argument? How did it work out?

→ Why should we avoid pointless arguments with people who just want to fight?

→ What are some other responses we can give to people trying to pick fights?

FROM KRISTIN:

I have an unbelieving family member. We've talked, debated, and hashed out beliefs, but it's been showing grace and sacrificial love that has softened her heart.

89.
Be Kind Online

In our culture we're living more and more of our lives online. We spend hours a day posting and hanging out on our social media accounts, many of which give us a measure of anonymity. It's getting easier and easier to say and send things online without having to face the consequences of our words.

Humans can be unnecessarily cruel. If you don't believe me, just search YouTube for your favorite singer and scroll through the comments. It's not enough for someone to dislike an artist's voice or song choice; they attack looks, insult intelligence, and slam anyone who enjoys the artist's music. They've turned their opinion into royal truth, and they suddenly feel entitled to bully others who don't share their thoughts.

The old slogan "If you can't say something nice, don't say anything at all" doesn't seem to apply to our words online.

But it should. Before you press ENTER or SEND, remember:

Your words online matter.

Your words online have the power to build up or tear down.

You'll one day be accountable for what you say, even if it's anonymous.

It's easy to say something unkind and hide behind a computer or phone screen, not seeing the hurt and pain caused by our words. The Internet has provided a place to bully without consequences.

There are appropriate times to be honest online, such as leaving a review or engaging (politely) in a discussion, but even those should be laced with gentleness and kindness. (And maybe some smiley emojis so people know you're not angry.)

Anonymity isn't a free pass to be cruel. There's a soul behind that screen name, a *living human* behind that device.

So when you're about to type something, remember: *your words online matter*.

-Kristin

FROM GOD:

"I tell you, on the day of judgment people will give account for every careless word they speak." (Matthew 12:36 ESV)

GO AHEAD—ANSWER:

→ Have you ever been the target of cruel or mean comments online? If so, how did it feel?

→ Have you ever said mean or cruel things about people online? Were there any consequences?

→ Why do our words online matter?

FROM KRISTIN:

Ask yourself the following question: Would I say this to someone in person? Then determine whether you should say it at all.

90.
Meet a Talking Donkey

Sounds crazy, doesn't it? But God sometimes works in out-of-the-box ways. And this is exactly how God worked in Balaam's life. Who's Balaam? We get the answer in 2 Peter 2:15 (NCV): "Balaam was the son of Beor, who loved being paid for doing wrong."

Weird, huh?

Balaam's story is found in the Old Testament book of Numbers. He called himself a prophet of God, but he actually made a living from cursing people and casting evil spells on them. He was steeped in the occult.

He was a living contradiction.

How can one call himself a prophet of God yet curse people and desire that harm come to them? Let's look at what the apostle James says about this kind of action: "Blessing and cursing come pouring out of the same mouth. Surely, my brothers and sisters, this is not right!" (James 3:10 NLT).

No, it's not right. It's sin. But we serve a God who loves us more than we can imagine. And when we sin, He will go to great lengths to get our attention so we'll repent and change direction.

Evil King Balak saw God's people (the Israelites) coming toward his country, and he was afraid. He knew that God had empowered them to conquer anyone who stood in their way to the Promised Land. So King Balak asked Balaam to curse God's people.

While Balaam was on the way to curse the Israelites, however, God gave his donkey the ability to speak. It's an amazing story, and you can find it in Numbers 22–23. This shows me that God will go to great lengths to get our attention!

So what's the lesson? When God tries to get your attention—listen! This is the only time we know of that God used a talking animal to get someone's attention, but it proves that He will go to extreme lengths to get us to listen to Him.

Don't force Him to go to the extreme. Most of the time when He wants our attention, it's to help us—by reminding us to obey Him. So when God tells you to do something, just do it. It's always beneficial to obey, but disobedience always costs.

—Susie

• •

FROM GOD:

"Give your entire attention to what God is doing right now." (Matthew 6:34 MSG)

GO AHEAD—ANSWER:

→ In what area of your life has God been trying to get your attention?

→ Does He want you to do something specific? Does He want you to carry your Bible to campus, invite someone to church, share your faith?

→ Is there something specific He wants you to change?

FROM SUSIE:

I'm amazed that the Creator of the universe wants a relationship with me so much that He'll use people, things, and circumstances to get my attention.

91.
Try Fasting

When people in the Bible really wanted God to know they were serious about something, they often fasted. This means they would go without eating. The fast may have lasted anywhere from one meal to several meals. In other words, it may have been a short-term fast or a fast that lasted a few days.

Christians still practice fasting today. It's a wonderful way to put aside something that's important to you so that you can instead spend that time praying and reading scripture. You don't have to fast food. I have a friend who went on a media fast for several days. Another friend fasted Facebook. I once gave up Coca-Cola for a year. For you it might be movies, coffee, Instagram, or a specific meal. But use the time you'd normally spend eating (or involving yourself on Facebook) in prayer.

People usually fast because they're in desperate need to know God's will about something, or because they want a specific prayer to be answered. God honors fasting. He always loves it when His children prioritize their time around Him. But don't think of fasting as a magical way to get something. It doesn't work like that.

You may think it's impossible to go without food for a day. But it's amazing how God will *physically* strengthen you through spiritual avenues found in His Word and in prayer.

Maybe you're having a difficult time choosing between two colleges to attend. You've prayed about it, talked through the advantages and disadvantages of each one, yet you still don't have the clarity you need. This would be a great time to fast—reading the Bible more intentionally and seeking God's specific direction.

People often give something up for Lent. But that's not the same thing as fasting. Fasting is denying yourself something important specifically for the purpose of spending that time in prayer and reading the Bible.

—Susie

FROM GOD:

Paul and Barnabas appointed elders for them in each church and, with prayer and fasting, committed them to the Lord, in whom they had put their trust. (Acts 14:23 NIV)

GO AHEAD—ANSWER:

→ Do you know someone who prays and fasts regularly? What difference has it made in their life?

→ What kind of difference do you think fasting would make in your life?

→ What would be the easiest thing for you to fast? What would be the most difficult thing to fast?

FROM SUSIE:

I once gave up walking Obie and Amos for a week. But it was just because I was tired.

92.
Determine to Persevere

Kristin already talked to you about the importance of persistence. Now I want to talk to you about a very close relative of persistence—perseverance.

We don't hear the word *persevere* very often. It's not very popular. It means to stick with something until you finish it. So it often involves dedication, fortitude, and commitment. I wasn't good at persevering when I was a child.

I'd start something and soon quit because I was bored or because I wasn't good at it. I'm glad my parents taught me how to discipline myself to finish a project, task, or hobby. If they hadn't, I would have stopped writing this book at #3.

To persevere also means to keep going even when things are really hard. Check out one of my favorite scriptures: "We are pressed on every side by troubles, but not crushed and broken. We are perplexed because we don't know why things happen as they do, but we don't give up and quit. We are hunted down, but God never abandons us. We get knocked down, but we get up again and keep going" (2 Corinthians 4:8–9 TLB).

When I hear about persecuted Christians in other parts of the world who refuse to renounce their faith, I'm encouraged to persevere. A friend recently told me of a missionary couple who were told by terrorists that if they wouldn't curse Christ, the terrorists would cut off their little boy's fingers. These Christians stood firm, and though they suffered this horrific act of persecution, God strengthened their faith and the faith of their son. That's perseverance.

It's not only important that we persevere with personal projects and with our faith, but it's also essential that we learn to persevere in prayer. A popular saying when I was a little girl was "Pray until you pray through." Often we find ourselves shooting up quick, one-sentence prayers to God and desiring fast responses instead of taking the time to pray—and keep praying—until our prayer is answered.

Perseverance takes time, discipline, and steadfastness. God

honors perseverance.

Learn to become a disciple who knows how to persevere through difficult times, impatience, and uncertainty.

—Susie

• •

FROM GOD:

Blessed is the one who perseveres under trial because, having stood the test, that person will receive the crown of life that the Lord has promised to those who love him. (James 1:12 NIV)

GO AHEAD—ANSWER:

→ Have you ever started something and not finished it? What was it? Why did you quit?

→ Can you describe a time when you completed a project even though you wanted to quit? How did you feel when you finished?

→ Why do you think so many people stop before they've completed something?

FROM SUSIE:

People who don't persevere are usually procrastinators. I'll tell you about that later.

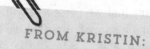

FROM KRISTIN:

Speaking of. . .I just realized we never finished that chapter on procrastination in our last book.

93.
Stay around People Who Sharpen You

"Iron sharpens iron, and one man sharpens another" (Proverbs 27:17 ESV).

Growing up, I used to watch my mom sharpen her kitchen knives by scraping them harshly against a long metal sharpener. It made an awful sound, and it didn't look fun for the knives. (In this particular analogy knives have feelings.)

In olden days, before we could go down the street and pick up almost anything at Walmart or Target, people crafted their tools and weapons by filing, heating, pounding, and refining the metal so it could be shaped, sharpened, and ultimately useful. Often they used one piece of metal to shape or sharpen another one. And the metal they used to sharpen the other piece was in some way different than the metal being shaped.

Just as metal was used to sharpen other metal, Christians sharpen each other when they're around one another.

Even more specifically, we become sharp by being around Christians who aren't exactly like us. Have you looked around your church? Every person there has unique likes, dislikes, gifts, and struggles.

We're sharpened when we learn to love and accept our Christian brothers and sisters even if they're different than us. This friction sharpens and hones us. When they're on fire for the Lord, it challenges us to learn and grow. When someone's struggling, it sends all of us to prayer on their behalf. If they disagree with something, we must learn to humbly address their concerns and issues without becoming bitter or angry.

Numerous times I've been around people who give generously, and as I've watched them live with open hands, I've realized that I, too, wanted to live with open hands. When I'm around people who see the good in others and encourage those around them, I become more encouraging myself.

You should intentionally spend time around people who love Jesus and are trying to serve Him with their lives. These people will sharpen you. Try and place yourself in a circle of people who will encourage you to grow in Jesus and call you out when they see you sinning.

It's nice hanging out with people who validate our every move, but we need people who love us enough to tell us when we're on a destructive path. Godly people will do this. They'll love, support, and encourage you, **but they'll also watch out for your soul.**

These people won't always be those you "click" with. In fact, your only thing in common might be that you both love Jesus Christ. You can learn a lot from those with whom you have little in common except your faith.

Lord willing, you'll find **a few new friends** with whom you share not just your faith but interests and passions as well.

-Kristin

• •

FROM GOD:

And let us consider how to stir up one another to love and good works, not neglecting to meet together, as is the habit of some, but encouraging one another, and all the more as you see the Day drawing near. (Hebrews 10:24–25 ESV)

GO AHEAD—ANSWER:

→ How are the people you hang around sharpening you?

→ How do you sharpen your friends?

→ Why do you think it's important that we hang around people who are different than us?

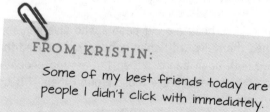

FROM KRISTIN:

Some of my best friends today are people I didn't click with immediately.

94.
Be the Salt

A massive chemical spill in West Virginia on January 9, 2014, left three hundred thousand people without clean drinking water. The chemical, MCHM, was released into the Elk River that runs through Charleston, West Virginia.

Can you imagine waking up to realize you can't brush your teeth, make coffee, take a shower, or get a drink of water because it's all contaminated? This specific chemical smells like licorice and can make it hard to breathe. It also causes headaches and irritation in the eyes and on the skin. The catastrophe was caused when the storage tank where the chemical was stored suddenly ruptured. One rupture affected three hundred thousand people!

On October 1, 2015, schools in Flint, Michigan, banned students from using water fountains because lead poisoning was found in the water.

In my small hometown of Bethany, Oklahoma, five thousand homes were without power in 2015 because of an ice storm that hit Friday night—the day after Thanksgiving—November 28. Nearly eighty thousand homes in Oklahoma City had no power. Trees, small as well as massive, split, fell, broke, and lined yards and even streets. I remember driving through the city and dodging branches everywhere on my way to meet a friend for lunch.

It's amazing what one act of devastation can do! Even a small mishap can affect great numbers of people.

On the other hand, a small act of kindness can turn everything around! I was in the post office around Christmas this year. The line was long, but there was only one woman in front of me. Her cell phone rang, and she politely moved out of line and into the back area to answer it. I was now next in line! The man at the counter was finishing his business when I saw the woman enter the room again and stand sadly at the very back of the line.

I smiled and motioned to her to come stand in front of me. "You were here before I was," I said. "Come get your place in line back!"

You would have thought I'd given her a million dollars. "Oh, thank you! Bless you," she said. "I really needed to take that call from my son."

I told her it was fine, but she kept thanking me until she reached the counter—and then she thanked me again!

We have a choice: we can decide to be salt and offer flavor to the world around us, or we can devastate others by a smug attitude, me-first agenda, and insistence on our rights.

Jesus told us in Matthew 5:13–16 that it only takes a small bit of yeast to make an entire batch of dough rise. Imagine putting a quarter cup of vinegar in your bread dough. Ugh! Just that one ingredient would make the entire loaf taste terrible.

Jesus not only calls us to be salt but also expects us to be light to the dark world in which we live. *You* can affect a lot of people! Determine to affect those in your life in a positive way.

—Susie

• •

FROM GOD:

"You are the salt of the earth. But if the salt loses its saltiness, how can it be made salty again? It is no longer good for anything, except to be thrown out and trampled underfoot. You are the light of the world. A town built on a hill cannot be hidden. Neither do people light a lamp and put it under a bowl. Instead they put it on its stand, and it gives light to everyone in the house. In the same way, let your light shine before others, that they may see your good deeds and glorify your Father in heaven." (Matthew 5:13–16 NIV)

GO AHEAD—ANSWER:

→ Describe a time when you were hurt because of the actions of another person.

→ What's the most recent act of kindness you've done? Describe the situation.

→ Have you ever affected a person (or people) in a negative way? What did you do to make it right?

FROM SUSIE:

Adding salt to my food enhances its flavor, just as an act of kindness enhances the flavor of life.

95.
Learn to Praise God

Have you ever thought about what it means to praise God? Psalm 96 tells us that someday the seas will demonstrate His glory, the earth will rejoice, and the fields will display His greatness.

Let that soak into your brain for a second. How will the seas demonstrate His glory? Will trillions of waves simply stand on top of the ocean's surface and begin to sing? Or will the plant life and mountains from the very bottom of the sea rise to the top and begin to shout, "Glory"? Will coral hum a praise tune?

Try to imagine how the very earth will rejoice. Will trees do hip-hop? Can you see a hill starting the wave? Maybe every blade of grass will boogie down to some rock and roll or the leaves will sing in harmony. Every grain of sand on the earth may belt out a brand-new praise song to the Creator.

And what about the animals? They're part of God's creation. You know they're going to be in on the action. I can't wait to hear it! Hippos, hyenas, hamsters, hawks, hedgehogs, hummingbirds, and horses may have their own "H Choir." And I can just hear the cats, chipmunks, cows, canaries, camels, chickens, cheetahs, crocodiles, caribou, chimpanzees, cobras, candors, crows, cranes, and even cockroaches trying to outdo them!

How do you personally praise your heavenly Father? I'm not talking about being in church and just singing what's on the screen because that's what everyone else is doing. I'm talking about personal praise that comes straight from your heart. It *may be* through singing or listening to praise music.

Though that's what usually comes to mind when we think of praise, there are other ways in which you can praise your Father. Try praising Him by kneeling the next time you pray. This is an act of humility and reverence. It shows that you revere Him as your absolute authority.

You can also praise Him vocally. When you're having your quiet time with God, interrupt the quiet by shouting, "Hallelujah!" or "I praise You, Lord!"

Another way you can praise God is by lifting your hands. This shows you're sending the praise in His direction. You're pointing toward the heavens. You're raising your hands in gratitude.

Try thanking God in prayer. This blesses Him. Yes, you can actually bless the Lord. In fact, it's scriptural! The proof is found in Psalm 103:1 (KJV): "Bless the LORD, O my soul: and all that is within me, bless his holy name."

We can only imagine what it will sound like someday to hear turtles, wildflowers, and caves praising our God. I can't wait to hear the melody of the stars singing in unison. The little ants will be singing soprano, and the queen bee will be singing bass. But we don't have to imagine what it's like for us. We have the privilege of praising God right here, right now. Let's do it!

—Susie

· ·

FROM GOD:

"All the earth worships you and sings praises to you; they sing praises to your name." (Psalm 66:4 ESV)

GO AHEAD—ANSWER:

→ How do you most often express your praise to God?

→ When was the last time you genuinely praised Him from your heart?

→ What's a new way you can start praising God?

FROM SUSIE:

I enjoy singing, but I also love to praise God by thanking Him for specific qualities that He has shown me of Himself. For example, I thank Him for His power that I've seen demonstrated in my life, and for His ability to be everywhere at once and always hear my prayers. I praise Him for His holiness, His grace, His mercy, and His compassion. I also thank Him for the fact that He is good, just, and fair.

96.
Learn to Relax

In the very first chapter of this book, we talked about how we're living in a hectic, fast-paced world. We want stuff not only fast—but immediately! Even minute rice is microwavable. Is this really necessary? I mean, if it only took a minute in the first place. . . .

God knows the importance of relaxing. Scripture tells us in Genesis 2:3 that He rested on the seventh day of creation. If God rested, don't you think it's important that we, too, learn how to relax and refuel?

How we relax is often determined by whether we're an extrovert or an introvert. Being around people is what energizes an extrovert. An introvert needs alone time to refuel. So if you're an extrovert, going out to dinner with friends will be exactly what you need. If you're an introvert, you may want to put a puzzle together, read a book, or simply cuddle with your pet in your lap.

I'm part extrovert and part introvert. I love people, and I enjoy being around them. But after awhile, I need some alone time. So I relax by watching *Wheel of Fortune* (because I joined the *Wheel of Fortune* Wheel Watchers Club and hope my number is chosen to win $5,000 at the end of the show) or a suspenseful movie, or even by taking a nap.

What relaxes you? Painting? Listening to music? Texting friends? Diving into Pinterest? Shopping? Whatever it is that relaxes you, carve some space out of your week to do it. We all need "me time."

Check this out: "Be still, and know that I am God" (Psalm 46:10 NIV). Our heavenly Father knows that when we're still, we can focus on Him more clearly. And when He reveals Himself to us, we tend to be still.

Most of us are microwave Christians. We have such fast lifestyles that the "hurry factor" carries over into our spiritual lives. We eat fast, move fast, talk fast, and drive fast, and now we want fast answers to quick prayers.

Maybe God wants to transform you into a Crock-Pot Christian!

Perhaps He wants you to slow down and just simmer awhile in His presence. Enjoy the aroma of His greatness. Allow His Word to cook slowly within your heart.

—Susie

• •

FROM GOD:

"Come to me, all you who are weary and burdened, and I will give you rest." (Matthew 11:28 NIV)

GO AHEAD—ANSWER:

→ What most relaxes you?

→ Do you refuel better with people or by yourself?

→ What's the most relaxing thing you've done in the past two days?

FROM SUSIE:

I'm totally relaxed when Obie and Amos are curled in my lap and all three of us are wrapped up in a blanket.

FROM KRISTIN:

I'm totally relaxed when I'm eating Chipotle and watching a comedy on Netflix.

97.
Be Safe in Your Car

Before I left for college (even though the university I attended was only a mile from my home), Dad thought it was important that I learn how to change a tire. I thought that was funny because I didn't even have a car! But he spent a Saturday morning with the tire jack and the spare and went through details such as loosening lug nuts and all that stuff. I pretended to be listening, but in my mind I was shopping for cool dorm decorations. The result was I still don't know how to change a tire.

That's unfortunate.

Because someday I'll probably have a flat tire. . .and yes, I can call AAA or a towing service, but sometimes it can take up to an hour for those people to arrive. And while I'm wasting precious time by the side of the road—and placing myself in danger—I *could* be changing the tire and leaving.

Even though I never learned this valuable lesson, Kristin and I want *you* to learn it. When you're in college, you'll make friends from around the nation. You'll probably take a few road trips, maybe drive somewhere fun during spring break, or visit friends in another state. Because the world is a much meaner place than it was in the 1800s, when Kristin and I were in college, you're setting yourself up for disaster if you're not prepared to take care of yourself on the road.

While you're learning how to change a tire, go ahead and learn all the basics about your car. I'm not talking about anything complicated, such as automobile restoration—or even changing the oil—just the basics. Let someone teach you how to open the hood of your car, recharge your battery, and check your oil.

Do you know where the spare tire is kept? Do you *have* a spare tire—and everything that goes with it? Do you have an emergency kit (if not, please create one; we'll go through this in a few seconds)? Keep your car manual, along with your proof of insurance and car ownership papers, in your glove compartment.

You can create a car emergency kit, or you can purchase one that is prestocked with everything you may need. A good emergency kit will include a charged cell phone, a first aid kit (with adhesive tape, gauze pads, aspirin, antiseptic wipes, antiseptic cream or ointment, and anything specific to your personal needs, such as an insulin injector or EpiPen), a fire extinguisher that's rated by the National Fire Protection Association for Class B and Class C fires, reflective warning triangles, a tire gauge, foam tire sealant, jumper cables, a flashlight and extra batteries, gloves, rags, duct tape, a tow strap or tow rope, a multipurpose utility tool, a rain poncho, bottled water, nonperishable snacks (such as protein bars), a blanket, a snow shovel and a windshield ice scraper.

Being prepared for the worst is simply being proactive to ensure your own personal safety and the safety of those in your car.

—Susie

· ·

FROM GOD:

Those who trust in themselves are fools, but those who walk in wisdom are kept safe. (Proverbs 28:26 NIV)

GO AHEAD—ANSWER:

➔ Have you ever been lost? How did you find help?

➔ Have you ever been in a car accident? Describe what happened.

➔ Have you ever experienced a disastrous situation that could have been avoided if you'd been more prepared? What did you learn from this experience?

FROM SUSIE:

I used to live in Colorado, and snowstorms often came unexpectedly. We could get snow as early as September and as late as June. It was simply foolish to even think about driving without having a couple of blankets in the trunk—just in case.

FROM KRISTIN:

I *just* moved to Colorado Springs and have never driven in snow. I'm prepared for the worst, though. I have a shovel, candles, matches, water, granola bars, Cheez-Its (getting stranded in a snowstorm would be much better with cheesy crackers), thermal sleeping bags, a flashlight, kitty litter for traction, tire chains, and a notebook and pen, just in case I get any creative ideas while stranded.

FROM SUSIE:

Now that I think about it, there might be such a thing as being overprepared.

98.
Call Someone

There's an easy way for you to make someone's day.

Are you ready for it?

Call them.

Your friends may prefer texting, but your mom, dad, aunts, uncles, and grandparents would be *thrilled* to hear your voice over the phone. (You probably still live with your parents, but tuck this piece of advice away for when you move out on your own. Call your parents!)

Back in the archaic 1990s, the only thing phones did was make calls. And most of the phones had to be mounted on the wall, so you had to talk to people in an area where other people were hanging out.

Times have changed a lot. However, your elderly relatives probably don't know how to text or use e-mail.

They do, however, know how to answer and carry on a conversation over the phone.

Talking on the phone is becoming a lost art, so let me explain to you how it's done. Don't worry, it's really quite simple: just listen into the earpiece to what the person on the other end is saying, and then respond. It's like magic!

Your grandpa, grandma, or other older friends and relatives will appreciate that you reached out and communicated with them using technology they understand.

–Kristin

· ·

FROM GOD:

"Remember the days of old; consider the years of many generations; ask your father, and he will show you, your elders, and they will tell you." (Deuteronomy 32:7 ESV)

GO AHEAD—ANSWER:

→ When was the last time you called someone?

→ What keeps you from calling people?

→ How do you think we'll be communicating by the time you have grandkids?

FROM KRISTIN:

I used to talk to my family a lot on the phone, and we always ended our conversations with "I love you, 'bye!" On at least one occasion, I said that out of habit to someone I was speaking to on the phone who barely knew me. (Like my banker.)

99.
Chase Wisdom

There's a character in the Old Testament of the Bible named Solomon. Solomon was the son of David. (If you've ever heard the story David and Goliath—*that* David was Solomon's dad.) Solomon became king of Israel, and God presented him with a very interesting offer: "What can I give you? Ask" (1 Kings 3:5 MSG).

Solomon could have asked for anything, and God would have given it to him. A long life, endless riches, adventure, security—you name it and Solomon could have had it.

Instead, do you know what Solomon asked God to give him? Wisdom.

More than anything, he wanted to be able to discern good and evil and have a heart for God.

Wisdom is being able to determine what's right. It's having unique insight to make the correct judgment about a situation.

Think about how handy it would be to know *exactly* what to say to a friend who is hurting. Or to know *precisely* what action to take when you see someone getting bullied. Or to tell *what* a person's motives are for asking you something.

Often in these moments we flounder. We don't know what's right. Perfect wisdom gives us the perfect response for any scenario.

That's why we should chase after wisdom.

How can we get wisdom?

First, we must ask. "If any of you lacks wisdom, let him ask God" (James 1:5 ESV).

Second, we must know what real wisdom looks like. "But the wisdom from above is first pure, then peaceable, gentle, open to reason, full of mercy and good fruits, impartial and sincere" (James 3:17 ESV).

Third, we must listen to sound instruction and be open to correction. "Listen to advice and accept instruction, that you may gain wisdom in the future" (Proverbs 19:20 ESV).

The entire book of Proverbs is filled with wisdom. It tells the differences between a wise man and a fool. If you're looking for a place to start, that's a good one.

-Kristin

• •

FROM GOD:

The beginning of wisdom is this: Get wisdom. Though it cost all you have, get understanding. (Proverbs 4:7 NIV)

GO AHEAD—ANSWER:

→ Do you know anyone who has a lot of understanding and wisdom? What are some of their traits?

→ When was a time when you've needed wisdom for something?

→ Why is it so important that we try to become wise?

FROM KRISTIN:

If you want to do a great wisdom project, grab a piece of paper and make two columns. Above one column write, "Traits of Wisdom," and above the other write, "Traits of Foolishness." Then read through Proverbs and write in the traits as they come up!

100.
Make Sure You Know

There are three really, really, really important decisions you'll make in life. Do you want to know what they are?

Deciding to follow Christ.

Deciding what to do with your life.

Deciding whom you'll marry.

The most important decision is to follow Christ. Following Christ means to realize that you were born a sinner. The Bible says *all* of us have sinned. Check it out: "All have sinned and fall short of the glory of God" (Romans 3:23 NIV).

Sin has a price—an extremely high price! Here's the proof: "The wages of sin is death" (Romans 6:23 NLT).

Bad news: You're a sinner.

Worse news: The cost of being a sinner is death.

Good news: God can forgive your sins and grant you eternal life! Proof: "If you declare with your mouth, 'Jesus is Lord,' and believe in your heart that God raised him from the dead, you will be saved" (Romans 10:9 NIV).

Even better news: When God saves you, He doesn't just save a little bit of you; He saves all of you! Proof: "He is able to save completely those who come to God through him, because he always lives to intercede for them" (Hebrews 7:25 NIV).

Bottom line: Someone has to pay for your sins. They're your responsibility, so you're in line to pay for them. *But* God loves you so much that He sent His one and only Son, Jesus, into the world to die a horrific death on the cross—to pay for your sins!

You don't deserve that.

You're not good enough for that.

You'd never be able to earn that kind of gift.

It's totally free.

You simply have to ask for it. And when you do, God wipes your slate clean. Salvation is a free gift. *Wow!* Amazing, isn't it?

But it's really more than just praying a simple prayer. Yes, it's His grace that saves us, but once we've been forgiven, it's our responsibility to obey Him, grow closer to Him, and share our faith with others.

Do you know for sure that you'll go to heaven when you die? If you're not sure, maybe you're not really a Christian. It's possible that you know *about* Christ but don't actually know Him personally. There is a big difference.

But you *can* know Him personally. It's important that you know for sure that you're a Christian. If you'd like to become a Christian, you can pray this prayer. These words aren't magic. You have to mean them. Pray from your heart. You don't have to pray this exact prayer; you can pray your own prayer and just use this as a guide. Or you can pray this exact prayer, but again, you have to mean it.

DEAR JESUS:

I believe You are who You claim to be—the Messiah, the Son of God. I confess that I'm a sinner, and I'm so sorry I've sinned against You. Will You forgive me? I don't want to live in opposition to You. I want to live *for* You. I believe You died for my sins. Thank You! And I believe the Bible is truth. Because You promised that You'd forgive me if I sincerely asked, I'm exercising my faith now. I believe that You hear my prayer and have chosen to forgive me. Thank You, thank You, thank You! I give my life to You, and I choose to live in obedience to Your will. I love You, Jesus. In Your name I pray. Amen.

—Susie

FROM GOD:

"Repent and be baptized every one of you in the name of Jesus Christ for the forgiveness of your sins, and you will receive the gift of the Holy Spirit." (Acts 2:38 ESV)

GO AHEAD—ANSWER:

→ How can you know for sure that you're saved from your sin? (If you prayed the above prayer or one like it, and if you're living for Christ, you're a Christian and have been saved from your sin.)

→ What difference has Christ made in your life?

→ Do you have a Bible? (If you don't, put this on your birthday list. You can get a version that you understand—and with cool graphics and scripture helps—from your local Christian bookstore.) If you have a Bible, read it at least one minute each day.

FROM SUSIE:

I became a Christian when I was nine years old. I've never regretted it. God is so faithful.

101.
Make Sure They Know

It's important that your friends and loved ones also know Christ. It's exciting to know that we can spend **forever** together with them and with Christ on the new earth! Do your family members know Christ? What about your friends? **Are they believers?** If not, would you be willing to share your faith with them?

You don't have to preach to them; that would turn them off. But you *can* lovingly share the wonderful **difference** Christ has made—and is currently making—in your life.

Become comfortable sharing your testimony. (If you need a refresher on this, reread #20, "Start a Spiritual Journal.") The more you share your testimony, the more natural it will feel. Pray that God will give you **specific** opportunities to do this so you don't have to worry about awkwardly trying to fit it into a conversation.

God will open the doors. For example, a friend may say, "How come you seem peaceful about stuff? That would've really made me angry." **That's an open door.** It's a perfect opportunity for you to say, "You know, I used to get angry a lot. But since I've gotten serious about God, He's made an amazing difference in my life."

Your friend is going to follow up on that. "What are you talking about?"

And you now have a **golden** opportunity to take it further: "He changed me from the inside out. He has given me a peace I never thought I'd have. He has also given me a purpose for life. He forgave my sins, and I know when I die I'll get to go to heaven and live forever."

"Doesn't everyone go to heaven? I mean, you just have to be a halfway good person, right? You know, not **murder** anyone."

"That's what a lot of people think. But the Bible says that the only way we can get to heaven is by having a personal relationship with Jesus Christ" (John 14:6).

And as you **continue** to relate your relationship with Christ, you can invite your friend to church or youth group, and you can even offer to pray with your friend so they can become a believer as well.

There's not a better feeling in the world than knowing *you're* forgiven and on your way to heaven—and knowing your loved ones are, too!

—Susie

● ●

FROM GOD:

Do not be ashamed of the testimony about our Lord.
(2 Timothy 1:8 NIV)

GO AHEAD—ANSWER:

→ Have you ever shared your faith with anyone?

→ Do you have a group of Christian friends who talk about spiritual things?

→ Will you write this verse on a card and place it where you'll see it often? Use it as a reminder of the importance of sharing your faith. "We are therefore Christ's ambassadors" (2 Corinthians 5:20 NIV).

FROM SUSIE:

There's nothing I enjoy more than talking about what God is doing in our lives when I'm hanging out with my Christian friends. And the next thing I enjoy most is having Mexican food with them.

About the Authors

Obie and Amos in the basket of Susie's bicycke.

Susie Shellenberger is a full-time speaker and writer who travels forty-two weeks/weekends every year speaking in churches, at universities, retreats, conferences, and camps. She is a former magazine editor, high school teacher, and youth pastor. Susie has written fifty-seven books, loves Trix cereal, and can sometimes be seen riding on her three-wheeled bicycle with her two schnauzers, Obie and Amos, in the rear basket. She lives in Bethany, Oklahoma. Find out more at SusieShellenberger.com.

Kristin Weber is a writer, speaker, and comic from Colorado Springs, Colorado. She wrote several years for *Sisterhood Magazine* and has contributed to many popular blogs. Kristin travels all over telling jokes and speaking about truth, culture, and identity to youth groups and at camps, conferences, luncheons, and more. Visit her online and be her friend at www.kristinweberonline.com.

Life Can Be Challenging for Teens. . . .

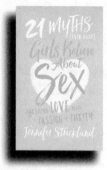

21 Myths Even (Good) Girls Believe About Sex
21 Myths (Even Good) Girls Believe about Sex uncovers the most believed untruths girls have about dating and sex. With honest, straight-forward language Jennifer Strickland shares the myths, the truths, and the practical ways young women can enjoy the pursuit of passion and purity.

Paperback / 978-1-63409-133-6 / $14.99

If I Could Ask God Just One Question
If I Could Ask God Just One Question is a much-needed resource for today's teens—whether they've grown up in the church or are new to the Christian faith. Eighty chapters, written in an easy-to-follow Q & A format, offer biblical answers to their most-asked questions about life, God, the Bible, and faith. Teens will come to realize that God isn't afraid of the hard questions and His Word has all the answers they'll ever need!

Paperback / 978-1-63058-351-4 / $7.99

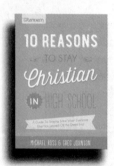

10 Reasons to Stay Christian in High School
Christian teens don't have to leave their faith back in Sunday school or slide toward what's popular (risking painful regrets). They can build the courage to "stay Christian" around their peers—and ultimately lead them to Jesus. This book is filled with everything they need to LIVE what they believe.

Paperback / 978-1-63058-375-0 / $7.99